Microsoft

MOS 2016 Study Guide for Microsoft Word Expert

John Pierce

Microsoft Office Specialist
Exam 77-726

MOS 2016 Study Guide for Microsoft Word Expert

Published with the authorization of Microsoft Corporation by:
Pearson Education, Inc.

ISBN-13: 978-0-7356-9935-9
ISBN-10: 0-7356-9935-6

Library of Congress Control Number: 2016953081

1 16

For information about buying this title in bulk quantities, or for special sales opportunities (which may include electronic versions; custom cover designs; and content particular to your business, training goals, marketing focus, or branding interests), please contact our corporate sales department at corpsales@pearsoned.com or (800) 382-3419.

For government sales inquiries, please contact governmentsales@pearsoned.com.

For questions about sales outside the U.S., please contact intlcs@pearson.com.

Editor-in-Chief
Greg Wiegand

Senior Acquisitions Editor
Laura Norman

Senior Production Editor
Tracey Croom

Editorial Production
Online Training Solutions, Inc. (OTSI)

Series Project Editor/ Copy Editor
Kathy Krause (OTSI)

Technical Editor
Joan Lambert (OTSI)

Compositor/Indexer
Susie Carr (OTSI)

Proofreader/Copy Editor
Jaime Odell (OTSI)

Editorial Assistant
Cindy J. Teeters

Interior Designer
Joan Lambert (OTSI)

Cover Designer
Twist Creative • Seattle

Contents

What do you think of this book? We want to hear from you!

Microsoft is interested in hearing your feedback so we can improve our books and learning resources for you.
To participate in a brief survey, please visit:

https://aka.ms/tellpress

What do you think of this book? We want to hear from you!

Microsoft is interested in hearing your feedback so we can improve our books and learning resources for
you. To participate in a brief survey, please visit:

https://aka.ms/tellpress

Introduction

The Microsoft Office Specialist (MOS) certification program has been designed to validate your knowledge of and ability to use programs in the Microsoft Office 2016 suite of programs. This book has been designed to guide you in studying the types of tasks you are likely to be required to demonstrate in Exam 77-726, "Word 2016 Expert: Creating Documents for Effective Communication."

><><><><><><><><><><><><><><><><><><><><><><><><><><><><><><><><><><><><><><><><><><><><>

Exam Strategy For information about the tasks you are likely to be required to demonstrate in Exam 77-725, "Word 2016: Core Document Creation, Collaboration and Communication," see *MOS 2016 Study Guide for Microsoft Word* by Joan Lambert (Microsoft Press, 2017).

><><><><><><><><><><><><><><><><><><><><><><><><><><><><><><><><><><><><><><><><><><><><>

Who this book is for

MOS 2016 Study Guide for Microsoft Word Expert is designed for experienced computer users seeking Microsoft Office Specialist Expert certification in Word 2016.

MOS exams for individual programs are practical rather than theoretical. You must demonstrate that you can complete certain tasks or projects rather than simply answer questions about program features. The successful MOS certification candidate will have at least six months of experience using all aspects of the program on a regular basis; for example, creating and modifying styles, building and inserting indexes and reference tables, customizing themes and style sets, protecting a document, and using advanced page setup options.

As a certification candidate, you probably have a lot of experience with the program you want to become certified in. Many of the procedures described in this book will be familiar to you; others might not be. Read through each study section and ensure that you are familiar with the procedures, concepts, and tools discussed. In some cases, images depict the tools you will use to perform procedures related to the skill set. Study the images and ensure that you are familiar with the options available for each tool.

How this book is organized

The exam coverage is divided into chapters representing broad skill sets that correlate to the functional groups covered by the exam. Each chapter is divided into sections addressing groups of related skills that correlate to the exam objectives. Each section includes review information, generic procedures, and practice tasks you can complete on your own while studying. We provide practice files you can use to work through the practice tasks, and result files you can use to check your work. You can practice the generic procedures in this book by using the practice files supplied or by using your own files.

Throughout this book, you will find Exam Strategy tips that present information about the scope of study that is necessary to ensure that you achieve mastery of a skill set and are successful in your certification effort.

Download the practice files

Before you can complete the practice tasks in this book, you need to copy the book's practice files and result files to your computer. Download the compressed (zipped) folder from the following page, and extract the files from it to a folder (such as your Documents folder) on your computer:

https://aka.ms/MOSWordExpert2016/downloads

> **IMPORTANT** The Word 2016 program is not available from this website. You should purchase and install that program before using this book.

You will save the completed versions of practice files that you modify while working through the practice tasks in this book. If you later want to repeat the practice tasks, you can download the original practice files again.

The following table lists the practice files provided for this book.

Folder and objective group	Practice files	Result files
MOSWordExpert2016 \Objective1 Manage document options and settings	WordExpert_1-1a.docx WordExpert_1-1b.docx WordExpert_1-1c.docx WordExpert_1-1d.docx WordExpert_1-1e.docx WordExpert_1-2.docx WordExpert_1-3.docx	WordExpert_1-1a_results.docx WordExpert_1-1b_results.docx WordExpert_1-1c_results.docx WordExpert_1-1d_results.docx WordExpert_1-2_results.docx WordExpert_1-3_results.docx
MOSWordExpert2016 \Objective2 Design advanced documents	WordExpert_2-1.docx WordExpert_2-2.docx	WordExpert_2-1_results.docx WordExpert_2-2_results.docx
MOSWordExpert2016 \Objective3 Create advanced references	WordExpert_3-1a.docx WordExpert_3-1b.docx WordExpert_3-1c.docx WordExpert_3-2a.docx WordExpert_3-2b.docx WordExpert_3-3a.docx WordExpert_3-3b.docx WordExpert_3-3c.xlsx	WordExpert_3-1a_results.docx WordExpert_3-1b_results.docx WordExpert_3-1c_results.docx WordExpert_3-2a_results.docx WordExpert_3-2b_results.docx WordExpert_3-3a_results.docx WordExpert_3-3b_results.docx
MOSWordExpert2016 \Objective4 Create custom Word elements	WordExpert_4-1a.docx WordExpert_4-1b.docx WordExpert_4-1c.docx WordExpert_4-2a.docx WordExpert_4-2b.docx WordExpert_4-3a.docx WordExpert_4-3b.docx	WordExpert_4-1a_results.docx WordExpert_4-1b_results.docm WordExpert_4-1c_results.docx WordExpert_4-2a_results.docx WordExpert_4-2b_results.docx WordExpert_4-3a_results.docx WordExpert_4-3b_results.docx

Adapt procedure steps

This book contains many images of user interface elements that you'll work with while performing tasks in Word on a Windows computer. Depending on your screen resolution or program window width, the Word ribbon on your screen might look different from that shown in this book. (If you turn on Touch mode, the ribbon displays significantly fewer commands than in Mouse mode.) As a result, procedural instructions that involve the ribbon might require a little adaptation.

Simple procedural instructions use this format:

→ On the **Insert** tab, in the **Illustrations** group, click the **Pictures** button.

If the command is in a list, our instructions use this format:

→ On the **Home** tab, in the **Editing** group, click **Find & Select** and then, in the **Find & Select** list, click **Go To**.

If differences between your display settings and ours cause a button to appear differently on your screen than it does in this book, you can easily adapt the steps to locate the command. First click the specified tab, and then locate the specified group. If a group has been collapsed into a group list or under a group button, click the list or button to display the group's commands. If you can't immediately identify the button you want, point to likely candidates to display their names in ScreenTips.

The instructions in this book assume that you're interacting with on-screen elements on your computer by clicking (with a mouse, touchpad, or other hardware device). If you're using a different method—for example, if your computer has a touchscreen interface and you're tapping the screen (with your finger or a stylus)—substitute the applicable tapping action when you interact with a user interface element.

Instructions in this book refer to user interface elements that you click or tap on the screen as *buttons*, and to physical buttons that you press on a keyboard as *keys*, to conform to the standard terminology used in documentation for these products.

Ebook edition

If you're reading the ebook edition of this book, you can do the following:

- Search the full text
- Print
- Copy and paste

You can purchase and download the ebook edition from the Microsoft Press Store at:

https://aka.ms/MOSWordExpert2016/detail

Errata, updates, & book support

We've made every effort to ensure the accuracy of this book and its companion content. If you discover an error, please submit it to us through the link at:

https://aka.ms/MOSWordExpert2016/errata

If you need to contact the Microsoft Press Book Support team, please send an email message to:

mspinput@microsoft.com

For help with Microsoft software and hardware, go to:

https://support.microsoft.com

We want to hear from you

At Microsoft Press, your satisfaction is our top priority, and your feedback our most valuable asset. Please tell us what you think of this book by completing the survey at:

https://aka.ms/tellpress

The survey is short, and we read every one of your comments and ideas. Thanks in advance for your input!

Stay in touch

Let's keep the conversation going! We're on Twitter at:

https://twitter.com/MicrosoftPress

Taking a Microsoft Office Specialist exam

Desktop computing proficiency is increasingly important in today's business world. When screening, hiring, and training employees, employers can feel reassured by relying on the objectivity and consistency of technology certification to ensure the competence of their workforce. As an employee or job seeker, you can use technology certification to prove that you already have the skills you need to succeed, saving current and future employers the time and expense of training you.

Microsoft Office Specialist certification

Microsoft Office Specialist certification is designed to assist students and information workers in validating their skills with Office programs. The following certification paths are available:

- A Microsoft Office Specialist (MOS) is an individual who has demonstrated proficiency by passing a certification exam in one or more Office programs, including Microsoft Word, Excel, PowerPoint, Outlook, or Access.

- A Microsoft Office Specialist Expert (MOS Expert) is an individual who has taken his or her knowledge of Office to the next level and has demonstrated by passing Core and Expert certification exams that he or she has mastered the more advanced features of Word or Excel.

- A Microsoft Office Specialist Master (MOS Master) is an individual who has demonstrated a broader knowledge of Office skills by passing the Word Core and Expert exams, the Excel Core and Expert exams, the PowerPoint exam, and the Access or Outlook exam.

Selecting a certification path

When deciding which certifications you would like to pursue, assess the following:

- The program and program version(s) with which you are familiar
- The length of time you have used the program and how frequently you use it
- Whether you have had formal or informal training in the use of that program
- Whether you use most or all of the available program features
- Whether you are considered a go-to resource by business associates, friends, and family members who have difficulty with the program

Candidates for MOS certification are expected to successfully complete a wide range of standard business tasks. Successful candidates generally have six or more months of experience with the specific Office program, including either formal, instructor-led training or self-study using MOS-approved books, guides, or interactive computer-based materials.

Candidates for MOS Expert and MOS Master certification are expected to successfully complete more complex tasks that involve using the advanced functionality of the program. Successful candidates generally have at least six months, and might have several years, of experience with the programs, including formal, instructor-led training or self-study using MOS-approved materials.

Test-taking tips

Every MOS certification exam is developed from a set of exam skill standards (referred to as the *objective domain*) that are derived from studies of how the Office programs are used in the workplace. Because these skill standards dictate the scope of each exam, they provide critical information about how to prepare for certification. This book follows the structure of the published exam objectives.

See Also For more information about the book structure, see "How this book is organized" in the introduction.

The MOS certification exams are performance based and require you to complete business-related tasks in the program for which you are seeking certification. For example, you might be presented with a document and told to insert and format additional document elements. Your score on the exam reflects how many of the requested tasks you complete within the allotted time.

Here is some helpful information about taking the exam:

- Keep track of the time. Your exam time does not officially begin until after you finish reading the instructions provided at the beginning of the exam. During the exam, the amount of time remaining is shown in the exam instruction window. You can't pause the exam after you start it.

- Pace yourself. At the beginning of the exam, you will receive information about the tasks that are included in the exam. During the exam, the number of completed and remaining tasks is shown in the exam instruction window.

- Read the exam instructions carefully before beginning. Follow all the instructions provided completely and accurately.

- If you have difficulty performing a task, you can restart it without affecting the result of any completed tasks, or you can skip the task and come back to it after you finish the other tasks on the exam.

- Enter requested information as it appears in the instructions, but without duplicating the formatting unless you are specifically instructed to do so. For example, the text and values you are asked to enter might appear in the instructions in bold and underlined text, but you should enter the information without applying these formats.

- Close all dialog boxes before proceeding to the next exam item unless you are specifically instructed not to do so.

- Don't close task panes before proceeding to the next exam item unless you are specifically instructed to do so.

- If you are asked to print a document, worksheet, chart, report, or slide, perform the task, but be aware that nothing will actually be printed.

- Don't worry about extra keystrokes or mouse clicks. Your work is scored based on its result, not on the method you use to achieve that result (unless a specific method is indicated in the instructions).

- If a computer problem occurs during the exam (for example, if the exam does not respond or the mouse no longer functions) or if a power outage occurs, contact a testing center administrator immediately. The administrator will restart the computer and return the exam to the point where the interruption occurred, with your score intact.

Exam Strategy This book includes special tips for effectively studying for the Microsoft Office Specialist exams in Exam Strategy paragraphs such as this one.

Certification benefits

At the conclusion of the exam, you will receive a score report, indicating whether you passed the exam. If your score meets or exceeds the passing standard (the minimum required score), you will be contacted by email by the Microsoft Certification Program team. The email message you receive will include your Microsoft Certification ID and links to online resources, including the Microsoft Certified Professional site. On this site, you can download or order a printed certificate, create a virtual business card, order an ID card, review and share your certification transcript, access the Logo Builder, and access other useful and interesting resources, including special offers from Microsoft and affiliated companies.

Depending on the level of certification you achieve, you will qualify to display one of three logos on your business card and other personal promotional materials. These logos attest to the fact that you are proficient in the applications or cross-application skills necessary to achieve the certification. Using the Logo Builder, you can create a personalized certification logo that includes the MOS logo and the specific programs in which you have achieved certification. If you achieve MOS certification in multiple programs, you can include multiple certifications in one logo.

For more information

To learn more about the Microsoft Office Specialist exams and related courseware, visit:

http://www.certiport.com/mos

Microsoft Office Specialist

Exam 77-726

Word 2016 Expert: Creating Documents for Effective Communication

This book covers the skills you need to have for certification as a Microsoft Office Specialist Expert in Microsoft Word 2016. Specifically, you need to be able to complete tasks that demonstrate the following skill sets:

1   Manage document options and settings
2   Design advanced documents
3   Create advanced references
4   Create custom Word elements

With these skills, you can create, manage, and distribute documents for a variety of specialized purposes and situations. You can also customize your Word environment to enhance the productivity you need to work with advanced documents used in a business environment.

Prerequisites

We assume that you have been working with Word 2016 for at least six months and that you know how to carry out fundamental tasks that are not specifically mentioned in the objectives for these Microsoft Office Specialist Expert exams.

The certification exams and the content of this book address the processes of managing, designing, and customizing Word documents and managing the options and settings that Word provides. We assume that you are familiar with the Office ribbon and that you understand basic Word features. This level of proficiency includes familiarity with features and tasks such as the following:

- Creating blank documents and documents based on templates
- Navigating through documents, including searching for text, inserting hyperlinks, and using the Go To command to find specific objects and references
- Formatting documents and text, including changing document themes, inserting simple headers and footers, and changing font attributes
- Inserting page, column, and section breaks
- Changing document views
- Printing documents, including printing document sections
- Customizing the Quick Access Toolbar
- Saving documents in alternate file formats
- Working with tables and lists, including using Quick Tables, applying styles to tables, and sorting table data
- Creating simple references such as footnotes and endnotes
- Inserting and formatting objects such as shapes, SmartArt, and pictures

Exam Strategy For information about the prerequisite tasks, see *MOS 2016 Study Guide for Microsoft Word* by Joan Lambert (Microsoft Press, 2017).

Objective group 1
Manage document options and settings

The skills tested in this section of the Microsoft Office Specialist Expert exam for Microsoft Word 2016 relate to managing document options and settings. Specifically, the following objectives are associated with this set of skills:

1.1   Manage documents and templates
1.2   Prepare documents for review
1.3   Manage document changes

In today's work environment, you often collaborate with coworkers and colleagues to write, revise, and finalize documents. Sharing documents within a group of users often entails specific requirements and tasks. You might need to track changes that reviewers make to a document, for example, or you might need to merge copies of a document that reviewers revised independently. In some cases, documents require the protection that a password provides so that only people with the password can open and modify the file. In preparing a document to use in a collaborative process, you might need to restrict who can edit specific sections of the document.

This chapter guides you in studying ways to manage documents, templates, and document changes, and ways to prepare documents for review.

> To complete the practice tasks in this chapter, you need the practice files contained in the **MOSWordExpert2016\Objective1** practice file folder. For more information, see "Download the practice files" in this book's introduction.

Objective 1.1:
Manage documents and templates

This topic covers a range of features that you use to manage documents and templates. It describes how to modify a template, compare and combine documents, copy macros and styles, move building blocks from one template to another, and link to external data from a document. It also describes how to manage versions of a document, enable macros, and set the default font that Word uses when you create a document.

See Also For information about creating building blocks and macros, see "Objective 4.1: Create and modify building blocks, macros, and controls."

Modify existing templates

One purpose of a template is to give related documents a common look and feel. Templates provide style definitions and can contain elements such as cover pages, custom headers and footers, themes, and macros. The components of a template help you create a document that meets a defined specification without needing to design the document from scratch.

To modify a Word template that you created or that you downloaded from the Start screen or the New page of the Backstage view, you first open the template file. After you open the template, you can modify it by creating styles, changing the properties of existing styles, designing custom headers or footers, and making similar types of changes.

Templates that you create are stored by default in the Custom Office Templates folder, which is a subfolder of your Documents folder. (Word opens the Custom Office Templates folder automatically when you select *Word Template* in the Save As Type list.) Templates that you download are saved in the AppData folder in your user profile. You can open this folder from File Explorer by entering *%UserProfile%\AppData \Roaming\Microsoft\Templates* in the address bar in File Explorer.

You can also modify a template when you are working on a document that is based on that template. For example, you can design a cover page for that template and then save that cover page as a building block. If you modify a template style while working in a document, you can apply the change only to the current document or to the template.

See Also For more information about creating and modifying styles, see "Objective 2.2: Create styles."

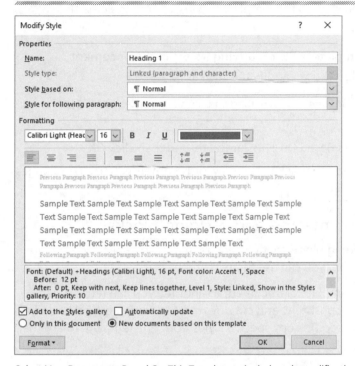

Select New Documents Based On This Template to include style modifications in the template

To open an existing template for modification

1. From the **Open** page of the Backstage view, browse to the folder where the template is saved (such as the Custom Office Templates folder or the Templates folder in the AppData folder of your user profile).

2. Select the template you want to modify, and then click **Open**.

Or

1. From File Explorer, browse to the folder where the template is stored.

2. Right-click the template, and then click **Open**.

To modify an existing template

1. Open the template.
2. Make the changes you want to the template's styles and other elements.
3. Save and close the file.

To update a document's template while modifying a style in the document

1. In the **Modify Style** dialog box, modify the style as required.

    > **See Also** For more information about creating and modifying styles, see "Objective 2.2: Create styles."

2. Select **New Documents Based On This Template**, and then click **OK**.
3. Save the document, and then click **Yes** when Word prompts you to save changes to the document template.

Move and copy styles, macros, and building blocks

The styles, macros, and building blocks that you create in one document or template can be copied or moved so that you can use them in others.

By copying styles from one template or document to another, you can reuse styles, keep related templates more consistent, and cut down on the work required to define styles in each template you need. To copy specific styles from one template to another, you use the Organizer dialog box.

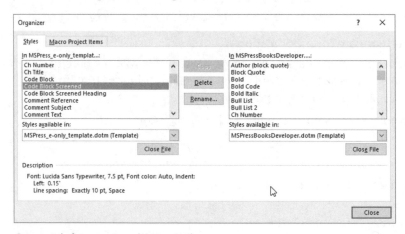

Copy a style from one template to another

The Organizer lists the styles defined in the templates (or documents) that you open by using the Close File and Open File buttons below the Organizer's list boxes. The attributes of a style you select in either list box are displayed in the Description area.

Read the description to determine whether you need the style in the template to which you are copying styles. In addition to copying styles from template to template, you can delete and rename styles in the Organizer.

You can also use the Organizer to copy macros between documents and templates. This is done on the Macro Project Items tab of the dialog box, which has buttons and list boxes that you can use to open the template or document that contains the macros you want to copy and the template or document you want to copy the macros to.

You can also move a building block, such as a header or a cover page, from one template to another. By default, the building blocks that are built into Word are stored in a template file named *Building Blocks.dotx*. Word stores this file in the *AppData\Roaming \Microsoft\Document Building Blocks\1033\16* subfolder of your user profile folder. (The folder named *16* stores files related to Office 2016.) The building blocks stored in this template are available to all the documents that you create.

> **See Also** For more information about building blocks, see "Objective 4.1: Create and modify building blocks, macros, and controls."

To move a building block to a different template, which makes the building block available in documents based on that template, you use the Building Blocks Organizer. The Building Blocks Organizer lists building blocks by name, gallery, category, and template. You can click the column headings to sort the list so that you can find the building block you need more easily.

To copy styles between templates

1. Open the **Styles** pane.

2. At the bottom of the **Styles** pane, click the **Manage Styles** button.

3. In the **Manage Styles** dialog box, click **Import/Export** to display the Styles tab of the Organizer.

4. In the **Styles available in** lists, click the templates you want to copy styles from and to. If the template isn't in the list, do the following:

   a. Click **Close File** to release the current template style list, and then click **Open File** to display the content of the Templates folder.

   b. In the **Open** dialog box, navigate to and select the template or document you want to use, and then click **Open**.

5. In the list box for the template you are copying styles from, select a style or styles, and then click **Copy**.

6. When you are done copying styles, click **Close**.

To copy macros between templates

1. On the **View** tab, in the **Macros** group, click the **Macros** arrow, and then click **View Macros**.

2. In the **Macros** dialog box, click **Organizer** to display the Macro Project Items tab of the Organizer.

3. Click **Close File** and **Open File** to display the templates or documents you want to copy macros from and to.

4. In the list box for the template you are copying macros from, select the macros, and then click **Copy**.

5. When you are done copying macros, click **Close**.

To move a building block to a document or template

1. Open the template (or a document based on that template) that you want to move the building block to.

2. On the **Insert** tab, in the **Text** group, click **Quick Parts**, and then click **Building Blocks Organizer**.

3. In the **Building Blocks Organizer**, select the entry for the building block you want to move, and then click **Edit Properties**.

4. In the **Modify Building Block** dialog box, in the **Save in** list, select the template where you want to store the building block.

5. Click **OK** in the **Modify Building Block** dialog box, and then click **Yes** to confirm the operation.

6. In the **Building Blocks Organizer**, click **Close**.

Manage document versions

Word uses its AutoRecover feature to save versions of a document as you write, insert content, and edit the document. You set the options related to automatically saving and recovering files on the Save page of the Word Options dialog box.

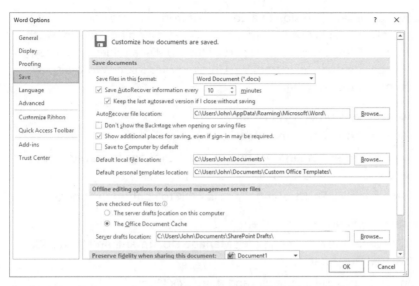

Configure AutoRecover options on the Save page of the Word Options dialog box

You can change the time interval for saving versions of your documents (the default interval is 10 minutes). You can also change the default AutoRecover file location, moving it from the AppData folder in your user profile to a folder that's more easily accessible, for example. By default, Word also retains the last version that it saved automatically if you close a document without saving it. (These settings apply only to Word and not to other Office programs.)

You can manage and recover versions of documents on the Info page of the Backstage view. Versions of the file that were saved automatically are listed under Manage Document. Right-clicking an item in the list displays options that you can use to open that version, delete the version, or compare that version with the current one.

When you open an autosaved version, Word displays a message bar telling you that the version is a recovered file that is temporarily stored on your computer. On the message bar, you can click Compare to view the differences between the version you opened and the last saved version. Clicking Restore overwrites the last saved version with the version of the document you opened.

You can also recover an unsaved version of a document from the Info page. Clicking the Recover Unsaved Documents option displays the Open dialog box and shows the contents of the Unsaved Files folder, which is part of the AppData folder structure in your user profile. When you open a file from the Unsaved Files folder, Word displays the Save As button on the message bar.

To restore an autosaved version of a document

1. With the document open, click the **File** tab.

2. On the **Info** page, under **Manage Document**, right-click an autosaved version of the file, and then click **Open Version**.

3. In the message bar, click **Restore**, and then click **OK** to confirm the operation.

To recover an unsaved version of a document

1. On the **Info** page for the document, click **Manage Document**, and then click **Recover Unsaved Documents**.

2. In the **Open** dialog box, select the file, and then click **Open**.

3. On the message bar, click **Save As**, and in the **Save As** dialog box, name and save the file.

Compare and combine documents

When you work with other authors and reviewers on multiple copies of the same document, you can collect the copies and then use the Combine command to merge the documents and produce a single document that displays and identifies revisions.

Other times you might simply want to compare two versions of a document to view how the versions differ. In this instance, you aren't concerned about who made revisions; you just want to know how the content in one version compares with the content in the other.

The Compare and Combine commands on the Review tab provide similar results when you merge documents, but you apply these commands in different circumstances. Use Compare when you want to view the differences between two versions of a document. Use the Combine command to merge revisions made in multiple copies of a document and to identify who made the revisions.

When you compare two versions of a document, the differences between the original document and the revised document are shown in the original document (or in a new document) as tracked changes. To get the best results when you use the Compare command, make sure that the original and the revised documents do not contain any tracked changes. If either document does, Word treats the changes as accepted when it compares the documents.

In the Compare Documents dialog box, you select the original document and the revised document, choose settings for the types of changes Word will mark, and specify whether Word shows the results of the comparison in the original document, the revised document, or a new document.

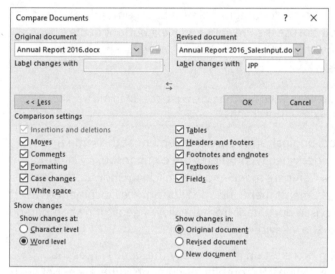

Clear check boxes of elements that you don't want to compare

By default, all the options in the Comparison Settings area are selected. You can clear the check box for any option other than Insertions And Deletions. If you don't need to view formatting differences, for example, clear the Formatting option. If you are interested chiefly in comparing the differences in the main body of each document, you might also clear the check boxes for Comments, Case Changes (whether a character is lowercase or uppercase), White Space, Headers And Footers, and Fields. In the Show

Changes area, Word Level is selected by default. Select the Character Level option if you want Word to mark when a change is made to a few characters of a word, such as when only the case of the first letter is changed. At the word level, the entire word is shown as a revision when the documents are compared; at the character level, only the letter is shown as a revision.

In the Show Changes In area, you can select Original Document to display the differences in that document (although you might not want to alter the original document in that way). Or you can select Revised Document to add changes to that document or New Document to create a document based on the original, with the differences made in the revised document shown with tracked changes.

The differences that are shown in the document created by a comparison are attributed to a single author. You can use the Previous and Next buttons in the Changes group on the Review tab to move from change to change, view the changes, and accept or reject the differences.

> **See Also** For information about accepting and rejecting changes, see "Manage tracked changes" in "Objective 1.3: Manage document changes."

You can also view the compared, original, and revised document at the same time (if that isn't the view Word provides when it completes the comparison) by clicking Show Source Documents on the Compare menu and then clicking Show Both. Other options on the Show Source Documents menu include Hide Source Documents (which removes the original and the revised document from the view, keeping the compared document), Show Original, and Show Revised.

The Combine Documents dialog box is set up in essentially the same way as the Compare Documents dialog box. When you combine documents, differences between the original and revised documents are shown as tracked changes. If a revised document includes tracked changes, these changes are also displayed in the combined document as tracked changes. Each reviewer is also identified in the combined document.

When you click OK in the Combine Documents dialog box, Word is likely to display a message box telling you that only one set of formatting changes can be stored in the merged document. You need to choose between the changes in the original document or the revised document to continue merging the documents. Word displays the results of combining the documents in a set of windows that shows the combined document in a central pane and the original and revised documents in smaller panes at the right.

Word also displays the Revisions pane along the left side of the window.

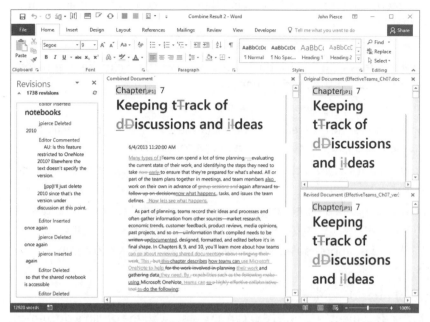

When comparing documents, Word displays the original, the revision, and a combined version

---

Tip In the window that Word displays after you combine documents, you can scroll through the combined document and the original and revised documents at the same time. Your location in each document is synchronized, so you can refer to any of the documents as you need to.

You can combine another copy of the document with the merged document by choosing Combine from the Compare menu again, selecting the combined result document as the original document, and selecting the next file you want to merge.

After you save and name the combined document, you can open that document and work through the variations (indicated by tracked changes), accepting and rejecting them to achieve a final document.

To compare documents

1. Do any of the following:

    -   Open a blank document.
    -   Open the original document.
    -   Open the revised document.

2. On the **Review** tab, in the **Compare** group, click **Compare**, and then click **Compare** on the menu.

3. In the **Compare Documents** dialog box, select the original document (if it isn't already selected) from the list or by clicking the folder icon and browsing to the location where the document is saved.

4. Select the revised document you want to compare with the original document.

5. In the **Label changes with** box for the revised document, specify the user name or initials you want to attribute differences to.

6. If the **Comparison settings** area is not displayed, click **More**.

7. In the **Comparison settings** area, clear or select the check boxes to specify the document elements you want Word to use in its comparison.

8. In the **Show changes at** area, choose whether to show changes at the character level or at the word level.

9. In the **Show changes in** area, choose where you want Word to show changes: in the original document, in the revised document, or in a new document.

10. Click **OK**. If Word prompts you about tracked changes, click **Yes** to complete the comparison.

To combine two or more documents

1. Open a blank document in Word. (You can also start with the original document or one of the revised documents open.)

2. On the **Review** tab, in the **Compare** group, click **Compare**, and then click **Combine**.

3. In the **Combine Documents** dialog box, select the original document (if it isn't already selected) from the list or by clicking the folder icon and browsing to the location where the document is saved.

4. Select the revised document you want to combine with the original document.

5. In the **Label changes with** box for the original and revised document, specify the user name or initials you want to attribute differences to.

6. If the **Comparison settings** area is not displayed, click **More**.

7. In the **Comparison settings** area, clear or select the check boxes to specify the document elements you want Word to use in its comparison.

8. In the **Show changes at** area, choose whether to show changes at the character level or at the word level.

9. In the **Show changes in** area, choose where you want Word to show changes: in the original document, in the revised document, or in a new document.

10. Click **OK**.

11. In the message box, specify whether to use formatting in the original document or the revised document.

12. Click **Continue with Merge**.

Link to external data

The tasks involved in managing documents can encompass not only working with multiple Word documents but also working with external data or files that you link to from a Word document. You can link to the content in another Word document and to files created in other Office programs or to Adobe Acrobat documents, for example. You can link to the content of the source file, embed the contents of a file, or display the file as an icon. You can also create an object (such as a chart or a slide) to insert in a Word document.

To link to external data, you use either the Object dialog box or the Insert File dialog box. In the Object dialog box, you can create an object by selecting the object type from a list. You can display the object as an icon instead of the full object; then, in the Word document, you can double-click the icon to open the object. By default, Word embeds the content of the file you select in the document. If you select Link To File, Word creates a link to the source file so that updates to the source file are reflected in the Word document. When you link to a file, Word displays an image of the file in the Word document. Double-clicking this image opens the source program.

In the Insert File dialog box, you can select a file to include in the current document. When you select the Insert As Link command to link to the file, Word inserts a field code by using the INCLUDETEXT field. This field creates a dynamic link to the source file so that updates to that file are reflected in the document in which you created the link. Be mindful that the INCLUDETEXT field uses the full path to the file you insert. If you move or rename the file you have linked to and then update the field, Word displays an error message indicating that the field refers to an invalid file name.

To link to external data

1. On the **Insert** tab, in the **Text** group, click **Object**.

2. In the **Object** dialog box, click the **Create from File** tab.

3. In the **File name** box, enter the name of the file you want to link to, or click **Browse** and then navigate to and select the file.

4. In the **Object** dialog box, select the **Link to file** check box, and then click **OK**.

To link to a file

1. On the **Insert** tab, in the **Text** group, open the **Object** menu and then click **Text from File**.

2. In the **Insert File** dialog box, click the file you want to insert.

3. Click the **Insert** arrow, and then click **Insert as Link**.

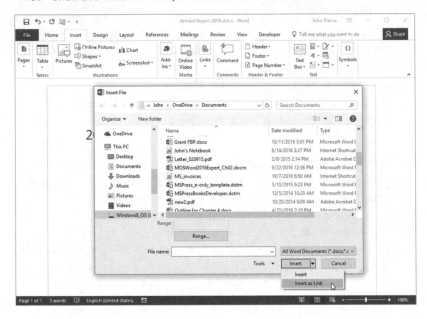

Choose Insert As Link to add a field to a document, linking to the content in the source file

Enable macros in a document

Macros can be used to automate operations and repetitive tasks in Word. For example, you can create a macro that applies a series of settings to an image that change the image's size and other formatting attributes all at once. Without the macro, you would need to select each setting separately.

Macros are created in a programming language known as Microsoft Visual Basic for Applications (VBA) and are stored in a VBA project that is associated with a document or a template. Because macros contain programming code, they can pose a security threat if the code they contain is malicious.

See Also For information about creating macros, see "Objective 4.1: Create and modify building blocks, macros, and controls."

To address this possibility, Word disables macros by default and notifies you with a security warning when a document you open contains a macro. You need to specifically enable the macros to use them in the document.

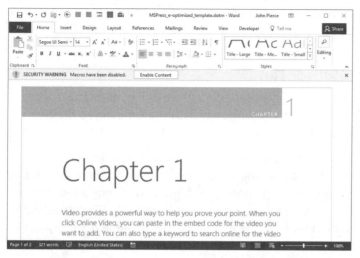

Word displays a security warning when you open a document that contains macros

In addition, you cannot save a macro in a document that uses the standard Word document format (.docx). When you start to save the document, Word displays a message telling you that the VBA project cannot be saved with the file.

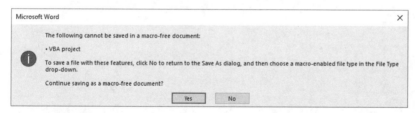

Use the macro-enabled file type when you save a document that contains a macro

To include the macro in the document, you need to save the file in the .docm file format, which is designed to include macros. Similarly, if you need to include a macro in a Word template, save the template in the .dotm format (for Word Macro-Enabled Template) instead of the standard Word Template (.dotx) format.

To enable macros in a document

→ In the message bar that Word displays when you open the document, click **Enable Content**.

To save macros in a document or a template

1. On the **File** menu, click **Save**.

2. In the **Save As** dialog box, in the **Save as type** list, select **Word Macro-Enabled Document (.docm)** or **Word Macro-Enabled Template (.dotm)**.

3. Click **Save**.

Change default program settings

There are many ways in which you can customize Word to make it meet your specific needs. Two common ways to do so are to change which tabs are displayed on the ribbon and change the default font.

The tabs that Word displays on the ribbon change when you work in different contexts and with different elements of a document. For example, when you select a table, Word displays the Table Tools tabs—Design and Layout. You can change which tabs are displayed on the ribbon yourself by choosing settings in the Word Options dialog box. Among the options are whether tabs that are hidden by default are displayed. The Developer tab is an example of a hidden tab that you can choose to display.

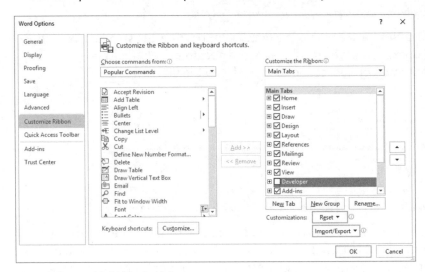

The Developer tab is hidden by default

When you set a default font, documents you create use that font and the settings you defined for it (font size, font color, and so on). Different templates can be defined to use different default fonts.

In Word documents, the default font is used in the definition of the Normal style and for styles based on the Normal style. The default font is also associated with the body font that is defined for the theme that is associated with a document or template. You can change the default font for a document or a template by specifying settings in the Font dialog box and then clicking the Set As Default button.

To display hidden ribbon tabs

1. On the **File** tab, click **Options**.

2. In the **Word Options** dialog box, click **Customize Ribbon**.

3. On the **Customize Ribbon** page, in the **Customize the Ribbon** list, select the check box for the tab you want to display. For example, select the **Developer** check box to display the Developer tab.

4. Click **OK** to apply your settings.

To change the default font

1. On the **Home** tab, in the **Font** group, click the dialog box launcher.

2. On the **Font** tab of the **Font** dialog box, select the options that you want to use for the default font.

3. Click **Set As Default**.

4. In the message box that appears, select whether to apply these settings to this document only or to all documents based on the current template.

5. Click **OK**.

Objective 1.1 practice tasks

The practice files for these tasks are located in the **MOSWordExpert2016 \Objective1** practice file folder. The folder also contains result files that you can use to check your work.

➤ Start Word and do the following:

- ❏ Use the Combine command to merge the **WordExpert_1-1a** and **WordExpert_1-1b** documents, using the default settings.

- ❏ Save the document in the practice file folder as <u>WordExpert_1-1_combined</u>.

- ❏ Open the **WordExpert_1-1a_results** document. Compare the two documents to check your work. Then close the documents.

➤ Use the Organizer to copy the *Practice tasks* style from the **WordExpert_1-1c** template to the **WordExpert_1-1d** template.

- ❏ Open the **WordExpert_1-1b_results** file, and then open the **Styles** pane and compare the style list to the one in your practice file.

- ❏ Open the **WordExpert_1-1c** template (right-click the file, and then click **Open**), and then modify the template by changing the *Practice tasks* style so that its font style is bold italic.

    See Also For more information about creating and modifying styles, see "Objective 2.2: Create styles."

- ❏ Open the **WordExpert_1-1c_results** file, open the **Styles** pane, and then view the modified style.

- ❏ Open the **WordExpert_1-1a** document, and then use commands in the Object dialog box to insert the text of the **WordExpert_1-1e** document after the first paragraph.

➤ Save the **WordExpert_1-1a** document.

➤ Open the **WordExpert_1-1d_results** document. Compare the two documents to check your work. Then close all open documents.

Objective 1.2: Prepare documents for review

Preparing a document for review can involve several steps. You might turn on change tracking and select options for how Word tracks changes and displays revisions. You might also need to restrict the editing of a document so that reviewers can only enter comments, for example, and not make changes directly to the text. You can also specify sections of a document that can be edited only by certain individuals.

See Also For more information about change tracking, see "Objective 1.3: Manage document changes."

Word also provides options to protect a document with a password and to mark a document as final, which notifies users who open the document that the document is considered complete.

This topic guides you in studying the steps involved in preparing documents for review.

When you share a document to obtain comments from peers or colleagues or for someone to make revisions to sections of the document, you don't want reviewers to modify the document at will by changing the formatting, adding or deleting content, inserting graphics, or making other modifications. Documents that contain important data or that you plan to use as the focus of a report or presentation can be protected before you share them. You can use options available in Word to restrict the types of changes users can make to a document, specify who can edit a document, and mark which sections of a document specific individuals can edit.

To control how a document can be edited, you set options in the Restrict Editing pane.

Use the settings in the Restrict Editing pane to allow specific people to edit all or part of the document

The pane has three sections:

- **Formatting restrictions** Select the check box in this area to limit formatting to a specific set of styles and to prevent users of a document from modifying styles and applying local formatting. From the Restrict Editing pane, you can open the Formatting Restrictions dialog box, where you can select the set of styles that is available to users working with the document. You can allow all styles or a set of styles designated by Word, specify that no styles can be applied, or select the specific styles you want to use.

The options at the bottom of the Formatting Restrictions dialog box control whether users can switch themes or substitute quick styles and whether settings for automatic formatting can override the restrictions you specify.

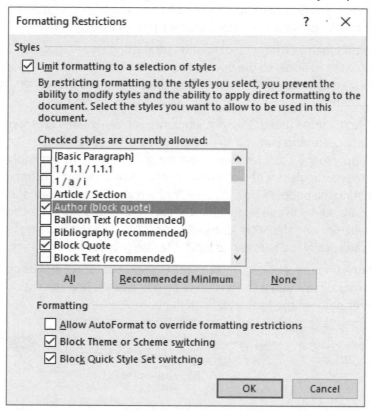

Select the styles and formatting options you want to allow in a document

- **Editing restrictions** Use the Editing Restrictions area to control the types of changes users can make to the document. The options include:

  - **No changes (Read only)** This prevents users from making revisions, although you can set up exceptions that allow specific users to edit all or certain sections of the document.

  - **Tracked changes** Revisions made to the document are indicated by revision marks. Tracked changes cannot be turned off without removing protection from the document, and removing protection can be controlled by defining a password.

  - **Comments** Users can add comments to the document, but they can't make revisions to the document's content itself. For this option, you can set up exceptions for specific users.

> **See Also** For more information about comments, see "Insert and manage comments" in "Objective 1.3: "Manage document changes."

- **Filling in forms** This option lets you restrict input to filling in form controls (such as check boxes and list boxes) that are part of a document.

- **Start Enforcement**   After you define the formatting and editing restrictions you want to apply to the document, use the Start Enforcing Protection dialog box to define a password that's required to remove protection from the document.

If you select No Changes (Read Only) or Comments, you can use the Exceptions area to specify users who can edit the whole document or sections of it. Exceptions apply to the complete document by default, but you can apply exceptions to a particular section of a document by selecting that section and then designating the people who can edit it. You can also allow everyone to edit specific sections, and you can apply different exceptions to different sections of a document. Clicking the More Users link opens the Add Users dialog box, where you can specify the names of people who are granted an exception.

If you specify editing exceptions, you and other users can locate and display the sections of a document that a specific user can edit by selecting the check box beside a user's name in the Restrict Editing pane.

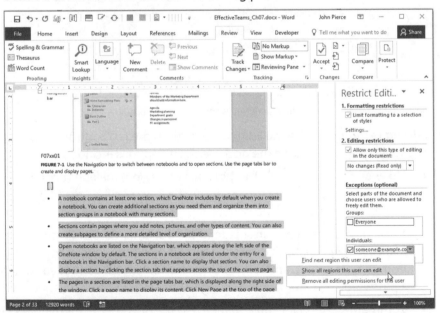

Use the menu to locate sections that a specific user can edit and to remove editing permissions

1

As a step in completing a document you have worked on with a group, you can mark the document as final so that colleagues or coworkers know the document's status. Marking a document as final provides a notification of its status; it does not prevent users from making changes (users can turn off the feature), and it does not provide the same level of protection as applying a password to the document.

When a user opens a document that is marked final, Word displays the message bar, notifying the user of the document's status. In addition, the title bar of the document window indicates that the file's status is read-only.

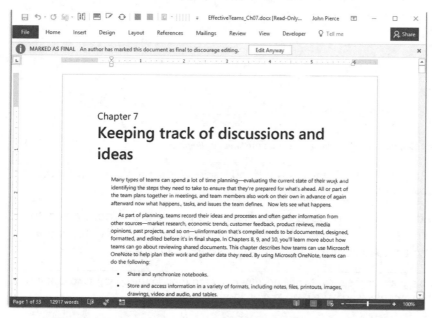

A user must intentionally activate the document to make changes

When you save a document from the Save As dialog box, you can display the General Options dialog box and then define a password that users need to enter to open the document, in addition to a password that's required to modify the document.

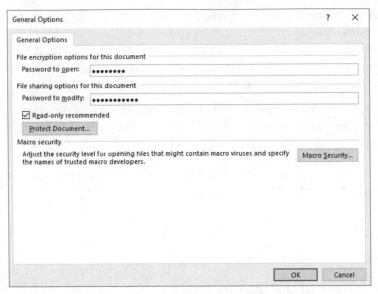

The General Options dialog box is available only from the Save As dialog box

---

IMPORTANT Be careful to retain the passwords you assign. Word provides no way for you to recover these passwords.

Keep in mind that requiring users to enter a password before they modify a document is intended to protect a document from unintentional editing. Defining this password does not encrypt a document to help secure it from malicious users.

Tip Encryption enhances the security of a document by scrambling the contents so that it can be read only by someone who has a password or another type of key.

To protect a document through encryption, you can use the Protect Document command on the Info page of the Backstage view. When you define an encryption password, Word cautions you that the password cannot be recovered.

To restrict editing and formatting

1. On the **Review** tab, click **Restrict Editing**.

2. In the **Restrict Editing** pane, select the options you want to apply:

   - To specify a set of styles users can apply, select the **Limit formatting to a selection of styles** check box, and then click **Settings**. In the **Formatting Restrictions** dialog box, select the set of styles and formatting options you want to make available in the document, and then click **OK**.

   - To control the type of editing allowed in the document, select the **Allow only this type of editing in the document** check box, and then choose from the options in the list. Define exceptions by selecting a section of the document and then choosing which users can edit the selected section.

3. Click **Yes, Start Enforcing Protection**.

4. In the **Start Enforcing Protection** dialog box, if you want to prevent other readers from removing the protection without permission, enter and reenter a password. Then click **OK**.

To mark a document as final

1. On the **Info** page of the Backstage view, click **Protect Document**, and then click **Mark as Final**.

2. Click **OK** to confirm the operation and save the document.

Tip Word might display a message box describing the effects of marking a document as final. Select the Do Not Show Again check box if you longer need Word to display this message, and then click OK.

To define passwords required to open or modify a document

1. In the **Save As** dialog box, click **Tools**, and then click **General Options**.

2. In the **General Options** dialog box, do either or both of the following:

   - In the **Password to open** box, enter a password for opening the document.

   - In the **Password to modify** box, enter a password for making modifications.

3. In the **General Options** dialog box, click **OK**.

4. In each **Confirm Password** dialog box that opens, reenter the appropriate password.

5. In the **Save As** dialog box, click **Save**.

To encrypt a file with a password

1. On the **Info** page of the Backstage view, click **Protect Document**, and then click **Encrypt with Password**.

2. In the **Encrypt Document** dialog box, enter the password you want to use, and then click **OK**.

3. In the **Confirm Password** dialog box, reenter the password, and then click **OK**.

To remove password protection

1. Open the **General Options** dialog box or **Encrypt Document** dialog box.

2. Delete the password that you want to remove, and then click **OK**.

Objective 1.2 practice tasks

The practice file for these tasks is located in the **MOSWordExpert2016 \Objective1** practice file folder. The folder also contains a result file that you can use to check your work.

➤ Open the **WordExpert_1-2** document, and do the following:

❑ Display the **Restrict Editing** pane.

❑ Configure the editing restrictions to permit only comments and no other changes.

❑ Set up an exception that allows users to edit the second section of the document.

❑ Start enforcing protection, and assign the password <u>WordExpert</u> to enforce protection (and to turn off protection when necessary).

❑ Encrypt the document content by assigning the password <u>WordExpert</u> to the document.

❑ Mark the document as final.

➤ Save the document.

➤ Open the **WordExpert_1-2_results** document, using the password *WordExpert*. Compare the two documents to check your work. Then close the documents.

Objective 1.3: Manage document changes

This topic describes how you can track and manage changes that you and other users make to a document. It covers how to turn on change tracking, accept and reject changes, lock change tracking, and add and manage comments. It also describes options for viewing changes and the comments added to a document.

Manage change tracking

The Track Changes command on the Review tab turns on or off the change-tracking feature. When change tracking is turned on, Word records insertions and deletions made to the current document's text, indicates where text was moved, and marks changes to formatting. You can set options for how Word displays tracked changes, and you can hide changes when you want to view a document in its altered or original state.

You do not need to turn on change tracking each time you open a document. After you turn on the feature, Word tracks changes to the document until you or another user turns the feature off. Having Word preserve the feature's status provides some assurance that important changes to a document will be recorded, but you can take an additional step to ensure that changes to a document are tracked by using the Lock Tracking option. In the Lock Tracking dialog box, you can define a password that people sharing the document must enter to turn off change tracking.

> **IMPORTANT** The password you define to lock change tracking does not secure the document against malicious users. It does not encrypt the document, for example. For more information, see "Objective 1.2: "Prepare documents for review."

As you revise and review a document with change tracking turned on, you can use tools in the Tracking group on the Review tab to change the view of a document to read it with more or less of the markup displayed. By using the Show Markup menu, for example, you can turn on or off the display of insertions and deletions, formatting changes, or comments. By selecting an option from the Display For Review list, you can view the document as though all revisions were accepted or as it was initially written.

> **See Also** For more information about viewing markup and setting markup options, see "Manage markup options" later in this topic.

Tracking revisions that you and other users make to a document can be simple and straightforward. When you click Track Changes on the Review tab, Word tracks the insertions, deletions, text moves, and formatting changes you make to the document. When you review the revised document, you can use commands in the Changes group on the Review tab to locate revisions and then accept or reject them.

You can also apply one or more options for how the program tracks and displays revisions and how you view them. In the Track Changes Options dialog box, use the check boxes in the Show area to specify which changes to a document you want to display as you work on the document. These options include Comments, Ink, Insertions And Deletions, Formatting, and others. You can also specify what information Word displays in balloons that appear along the side of a document in specific views. You can use balloons to view each revision or to view only comments and formatting changes. You can choose an option (Nothing) to view all changes inline. If you select Comments And Formatting, Word displays insertions and deletions in line within the document's text.

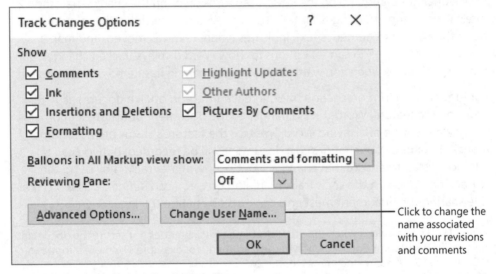

Click to change the name associated with your revisions and comments

Select the changes to display inline and in balloons

Tip Changes you make to a document are identified by the user name and initials shown in the Word Options dialog box. (The default user name and initials are created when you install Office.) For some documents, you might want to be identified by your role or with a user name other than the one currently set. For example, you might want to associate revisions with the name of your department if you are reviewing a document on the department's behalf. Click Change User Name in the Track Changes Options dialog box, and then enter the user name and initials you want to use. You also need to select the option Always Use These Values Regardless Of Sign In To Office—otherwise, comments will always be identified by using the name associated with your account. Any change you make to your user name and initials or to the setting for the Always Use These Values Regardless Of Sign In To Office option is carried over to other documents and to other Office programs. You should revert to your standard user name when you want to use it again.

The Advanced Options button in the Track Changes Options dialog box opens a dialog box where you can specify additional settings for how changes are tracked and displayed.

Advanced options include formatting of insertions and deletions and whether to track text movement and formatting changes

In this dialog box, you can do the following:

- Select the formatting that Word applies to insertions and deletions. By default, Word underlines insertions and uses strikethrough formatting to identify deletions. Other settings include Bold, Italic, Double Underline, and Color Only.

- Specify where Word places a line that indicates where a change was made. The default setting is Outside Border. Other settings are Right Border, Left Border, and None.

- Select a color to identify your changes. By default, Word uses the By Author setting, which means that Word assigns a color to each reviewer. You can select a specific color in which to display your changes.

- Select a background color for comment balloons.

- Specify whether Word tracks text that is moved. You can select the formatting (including the color) that Word applies to moved text in its original and new locations. If you clear the Track Moves check box, Word treats moved text as it does deletions and insertions.

- Set options for how changes to table cells are highlighted.

- Specify whether to track changes to formatting and how Word displays those changes.

- Specify the size and position of comment balloons. You can also specify whether Word shows a line that connects a balloon to the text it refers to.

- Specify how Word orients the page when you print a document with revisions and comments.

To turn change tracking on or off

→ On the **Review** tab, in the **Tracking** group, click the **Track Changes** button.

→ On the **Review** tab, in the **Tracking** group, click the **Track Changes** arrow, and then click **Track Changes**.

→ Press **Ctrl+Shift+E**.

To lock change tracking

1. On the **Review** tab, in the **Tracking** group, click the **Track Changes** arrow, and then click **Lock Tracking**.

2. In the **Lock Tracking** dialog box, enter and reenter the password you want to assign. Then click **OK**.

To unlock change tracking

1. On the **Review** tab, in the **Tracking** group, click **Track Changes**, and then click **Lock Tracking**.

2. In the **Unlock Tracking** dialog box, enter the password, and then click **OK**.

To set tracking options

1. On the **Review** tab, in the **Tracking** group, click the dialog box launcher.

2. In the **Track Changes Options** dialog box, do the following:

   a. In the **Show** section, select the check boxes of the types of changes you want Word to display as you work on the document.

   b. In the **Balloons in All Markup view show** list, click the information you want Word to display in balloons.

   c. In the **Reviewing Pane** list, click **Off** or **On** to indicate whether to display the Reviewing pane.

3. Click **Advanced Options**. In the **Advanced Track Changes Options** dialog box, do the following:

   a. If you don't want Word to track text movement, clear the **Track moves** check box.

   b. If you don't want Word to track formatting changes, clear the **Track formatting** check box.

   c. In each active list, click the formatting you want to assign to that type of change tracking.

4. Click **OK** in each of the open dialog boxes.

Manage markup options

When you are working on a document with change tracking turned on, you can use the Show Markup menu in the Tracking group to control the types of changes Word displays. Several of the options on the menu are the same as those provided in the Track Changes Options dialog box. For example, you can show or hide formatting changes, insertions and deletions, or comments by using the menu or the dialog box.

You can also use the Show Markup options to control what information Word displays in balloons in certain document views. You can show revisions in balloons or inline, or you can choose to show only formatting changes and comments in balloons.

Use the Specific People item on the Show Markup menu to view changes made by a specific reviewer or a subset of reviewers, instead of all reviewers, which is the view Word displays by default. If you display changes made by a specific reviewer or a set of reviewers, use the Accept All Changes Shown and Reject All Changes Shown commands to act on that set of changes in a single step.

> **See Also** For more information about accepting and rejecting changes and about the Track Changes Options dialog box, see "Manage tracked changes" later in this topic.

Word uses the term *markup* to describe the set of changes tracked in a document. As part of managing the changes in a document, you can use the Display For Review list in the Tracking group on the Review tab to switch between different views of the marked-up document. You can view the document as it was originally written, without any markup, or with some or all of the markup displayed. The choices are as follows:

- **Simple Markup** Word displays this view by default. With Simple Markup selected, Word displays the document as though insertions and deletions were accepted and displays a vertical line to mark areas of the document that include revisions. You can click that line to switch to All Markup view so that Word displays the markup. When Simple Markup is selected, comments added to a document are displayed as a small balloon that you can click to display the full comment. Click Show Comments in the Comments group to expand the display of all comments in the document.

- **All Markup** Select All Markup to display all the changes in a document, including inserted and deleted text, text moves, ink changes, and formatting changes. Word displays the marked-up document by using the settings specified in the Track Changes Options and Advanced Track Changes Options dialog boxes. For example, full comments and formatting changes are displayed in balloons if you specified that setting. In the All Markup view, you can control the types of changes Word displays and view the changes made by specific reviewers by using the Show Markup menu.

> **See Also** For information about options for tracked changes, see "Manage change tracking" earlier in this topic.

- **No Markup** Select this option to view the document as though all changes have been accepted. Word does not display a line indicating the location of revisions.

- **Original** Select this option to view the document as it was initially written—as though all insertions, deletions, and text moves have been rejected. (Formatting changes, however, are retained.)

To display specific types of markup elements

1. On the **Review** tab, in the **Tracking** group, click **Show Markup**.
2. On the **Show Markup** menu, click to remove the check mark next to any markup element you want to hide.

To display changes by specific reviewers

1. On the **Review** tab, in the **Tracking** group, click **Show Markup**.
2. On the **Show Markup** menu, click **Specific People**, and then click **All Reviewers** to hide changes from all reviewers.
3. On the **Show Markup** menu, click **Specific People**, and then click the name of the reviewer whose changes you want to view. Repeat this step to view changes by additional viewers.

To change the version of the markup that is displayed

→ On the **Review** tab, in the **Tracking** group, in the **Display For Review** list, click **Simple Markup**, **All Markup**, **No Markup**, or **Original**.

Manage tracked changes

When you review a document that includes tracked changes, you work with the commands and options in the Changes group on the Review tab or in the Reviewing pane (which is labeled Revisions when it is displayed).

By using commands in the Changes group, you can move to the previous or next change and then accept or reject that change or use options on the Accept and Reject menus to act on a change and move immediately to the next change. The Accept and Reject menus also provide options that you can use to accept or reject only the changes shown, accept or reject all changes in the document, and accept or reject all changes and at the same time turn off change tracking.

When the Reviewing pane is displayed, Word displays tracked changes in a list, labeling each revision as an insertion, deletion, or formatting change and indicating the name of the user who made the change. You can view revisions made by a specific person or persons by using the Specific People command in the Show Markup menu in the Tracking group.

See Also For information about viewing changes by specific people, see "Manage markup options" earlier in this topic.

To accept or reject a change

1. On the **Review** tab, in the **Changes** group, click **Previous** or **Next** to locate the change.

2. In the **Changes** group, click **Accept** to incorporate the change, or click **Reject** to remove it.

To accept or reject only changes that are shown

1. Set the markup options to display only the changes that you want to accept or reject.

2. On the **Review** tab, in the **Changes** group, do either of the following:

   - Click **Accept**, and then click **Accept All Changes Shown**.
   - Click **Reject**, and then click **Reject All Changes Shown**.

To accept or reject all changes

➜ On the **Review** tab, in the **Changes** group, do either of the following:

   - Click the **Accept** arrow, and then click **Accept All Changes**.
   - Click the **Reject** arrow, and then click **Reject All Changes**.

To display the Reviewing pane

➜ On the **Review** tab, in the **Tracking** group, click the **Reviewing Pane** arrow, and then select **Reviewing Pane Vertical** or **Reviewing Pane Horizontal** (depending on which orientation you prefer).

To accept or reject changes in the Reviewing pane

➜ In the **Reviewing** pane, right-click a revision (such as an insertion or deletion), and then use the **Accept** and **Reject** commands on the menu to accept or reject the change.

Insert and manage comments

Comments are a tool for reviewing and annotating a document. You can use comments to do the following:

- Highlight text or other content that needs to be revised or reformatted.
- Pose a question or seek clarification.
- Describe decisions to other reviewers of the document.
- Provide context or instructions for users of the document.

Word marks each comment that's inserted in a document with the name of the user who inserted it (or uses another identifying label; for example, a generic term such as Editor). When you point to a comment, Word displays information such as when the comment was inserted.

Depending on the current document view (Print Layout or Draft, for example) comments appear either in a pane along the side of a document, in the Revisions pane, or in ScreenTips. Comments are displayed in the Comments pane in the Print Layout, Read Mode, and Web Layout views. In Draft and Outline views, comments are displayed in ScreenTips when you point to the highlighted text. In any view (except Read Mode), you can display the Revisions pane to display comments. In Read Mode view, comments appear initially as comment icons. You can click an icon to read the comment. If you want to display the text of a comment instead of the icon in Read Mode view, you can click Show Comments on the View menu.

Tip The setting you select in the Display For Review list in the Tracking group also affects how comments are displayed. For details, see "Manage markup options" earlier in this topic.

By using the Balloons command on the Show Markup menu (or options in the Track Changes Options dialog box), you can choose an option to view comments (and other revisions) inline instead of in balloons. In the Track Changes Options dialog box, for example, select Nothing from the Balloons In All Markup View Show list to display comments inline.

You can move directly between comments in a document, and you can reply directly to a comment. At the bottom of the active comment balloon, Word displays the Reply and the Resolve buttons.

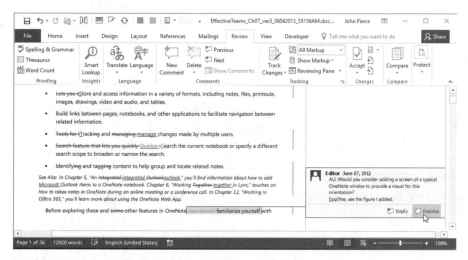

Resolving a comment indicates that its purpose has been fulfilled

When you reply to a comment, Word inserts the reply following the original comment. Replies are labeled with the user name and timestamp, and indented below the original comment. By resolving a comment, you indicate that the action or recommendation specified in the comment is complete or no longer active. In a document with numerous comments, marking comments as resolved helps you keep track of which comments are complete and which are active. When you resolve a comment, Word changes the comment text and label to a light gray. You can reopen a resolved comment if its content becomes relevant again.

You can also manage comments by using options on the menu that Word displays when you right-click a comment balloon:

- **Reply To Comment** Inserts a comment below the original comment (or below replies entered previously)

- **Delete Comment** Removes the comment from the document

- **Resolve Comment** Dims the display of the comment's text to indicate that the comment has been reviewed

If you want to emphasize the text in a comment, you can apply a limited range of font formatting from the Home tab or the Mini Toolbar. For example, you can apply bold or italic to text in a comment, highlight a comment, and change the font and font color. You cannot, however, change the size of the font.

To insert a comment

→ On the **Review** tab, in the **Comments** group, click **New Comment**, and then enter the comment. Depending on which document view you are using, you enter the comment in a balloon or in the Reviewing pane.

To move from comment to comment

→ On the **Review** tab, in the **Comments** group, click **Next** or **Previous**.

To delete a comment

→ Select the comment you want to delete, and then do either of the following:

- On the **Review** tab, in the **Comments** group, click **Delete**.

- Right-click the comment, and then click **Delete Comment**.

To delete all comments in a document

→ On the **Review** tab, in the **Comments** group, click the **Delete** arrow, and then click **Delete all Comments in Document**.

To reply to a comment

1. Select the comment you want to reply to.

2. Do either of the following, and then enter the reply text:

   - In the comment balloon, click **Reply**.

   - On the **Review** tab, click **New Comment**.

Objective 1.3 practice tasks

The practice file for these tasks is located in the **MOSWordExpert2016 \Objective1** practice file folder. The folder also contains a result file that you can use to check your work.

➤ Open the **WordExpert_1-3** document and do the following:

- ❏ Turn on change tracking
- ❏ At the end of the first paragraph, insert the text <u>The quick brown fox jumps over the lazy dog.</u>
- ❏ Move the second paragraph so that it comes after the third paragraph.
- ❏ In the fourth paragraph, delete the first sentence ("Themes and styles also help keep your document coordinated.")
- ❏ Select the option to format insertions with a double underline.
- ❏ At the start of the third paragraph, insert the text <u>Actions speak louder than words.</u>
- ❏ Select the option for balloons to show all revisions.
- ❏ Insert a comment related to the document's title. In the comment, enter the text <u>Please verify</u>.
- ❏ Mark the comment already in the file as resolved.
- ❏ Accept the revision you made to the first paragraph. Reject the deletion of the second sentence in the first paragraph.

➤ Save the document.

➤ Open the **WordExpert_1-3_results** document. Compare the two documents to check your work. Then close the documents.

Objective group 2
Design advanced documents

The skills tested in this section of the Microsoft Office Specialist Expert exam for Microsoft Word 2016 relate to designing advanced documents. Specifically, the following objectives are associated with this set of skills:

2.1 Perform advanced editing and formatting

2.2 Create styles

This chapter guides you in studying the ways in which you can edit and format longer, more complex documents, such as books, dissertations, reports, and requests for proposals. To begin, this chapter explains some of the advanced editing and formatting features in Word, including how to use wildcards or special characters to search for patterns in text, how to find and replace styles and formatting, and how to work with advanced page layout options such as document sections and text boxes. This chapter also describes how to create and modify styles so that you can more easily format a long document and keep the document's appearance consistent.

To complete the practice tasks in this chapter, you need the practice files contained in the **MOSWordExpert2016\Objective2** practice file folder. For more information, see "Download the practice files" in this book's introduction.

Objective 2.1: Perform advanced editing and formatting

This topic explains how to work with advanced editing and formatting features. It describes how to extend find-and-replace operations by using wildcard characters and how to use special characters when you search for and replace text. It next describes how you can carry out find-and-replace operations by using styles or specific format-ting. It also describes advanced page layout options, including how to insert document sections, add line numbers, and control hyphenation. Later topics in this section describe how to link text boxes, set paragraph pagination options, and manage conflicts that can occur when you copy formatted text from one document to another.

Find and replace text by using wildcards and special characters

Simple find-and-replace operations in Word can be extended in several ways. For example, in the Find And Replace dialog box, you can select an option to search only for whole words, use a case-specific search (*they're* instead of *They're*), or search by using how words sound (*they're*, *their*, and *there*). This section describes another way to extend find-and-replace operations—by using wildcard characters and special characters.

> **See Also** For more information about finding and replacing formatting and styles, see "Find and replace formatting and styles" later in this topic.

Use wildcard characters to find and replace text

You can extend your use of the Find And Replace dialog box by using wildcards. For example, as a wildcard character, the asterisk (*) represents a sequence of one or more characters. The question mark (?) is used to represent a single character within a sequence. When you combine wildcard characters with literal characters, you can find patterns of text.

The following table lists wildcard characters and examples of how to use them.

Wildcard character	Syntax and examples
?	Locates any single character. For example, *l?w* locates the words *law* and *low* and this sequence of characters in words such as *below* or lawful.
*	Locates a string of characters. For example, *J*n* finds *John*, *Jocelyn*, and *Johnson*. Wildcard character sequences are case-sensitive. To find *joinery* and journey, you would use *j*n*.
<	Finds characters at the start of a word. For example, *<plen* finds *plenty*, *plentiful*, and plentitude. It does not find the word *splendid*.
>	Finds characters at the end of a word. For example, *ful>* finds *fanciful*, *useful*, and *plentiful*. It does not find *fulfill* or *wonderfully*.
[ ]	Finds one of the characters within a sequence you specify. For example, *h[eor]s* finds words such as *ghosts*, *these*, *hose*, *those*, and *searches*, or the abbreviation *hrs* (hours). It does not find *horse*.
[n-n]	Finds any single character within the range you specify. You must specify the range in ascending order (*d-l*, for example). For instance, *[c-h]ave* finds *gave*, *have*, and *leave*.
[!n-n]	Finds any single character except the characters in the range you specify. For example, *st[!n-z]ck* finds *stack* and *stick* but not *stock* or *stuck*.
{n}	Finds the specified number of instances of the previous character or expression. For example, *cre{2}d* finds *creed* (two instances of *e*) but does not find *credential*.
{n,}	Finds at least the specified number of instances of the preceding character or expression. For example, *cre{1,}d* finds both *creed* and *credential*.
{n,m}	Finds the number of instances of the preceding character or expression in a range. For example, *50{1,3}* finds *50*, *500*, and *5000*.
@	Finds one or more instances of the preceding character or expression. For example, *bal@** finds *balloon* and *balcony*.
[\wildcard character]	Finds instances of the specified wildcard character. For example, *[*]* finds all asterisk wildcard characters.

As shown in the example for the @ symbol, you can combine wildcard characters to create expressions. For example, the expression *s[a-n]{2}d* finds words such as *send*, *sending*, *dashed*, and *slide*, but it does not find the word *sad*. In this expression, Word searches for a string of characters that starts with *s*, contains two characters within the range *a-n*, and ends with *d*. You can also use parentheses to group wildcard characters and text to indicate the order of evaluation. For example, the expression *<(det)*(ing)>* finds *determining* and *deterring*, with the character sequence *det* at the start of the word (indicated by the < symbol) and the sequence *ing* at the end (indicated by the > symbol). Keep in mind that all searches in which you use wildcards are case-specific. As an example, the expression *[c-h]ave* finds *have* and *cave* but not the name *Dave*.

> **Tip** When the Use Wildcards option is selected in the Find And Replace dialog box, the wildcard characters you can use appear on the Special menu. You can then select a character or enter the character or characters you want to use in the Find What and Replace With boxes.

You can also use wildcards to replace patterns of text. For example, you can use the \n wildcard character to invert first and last names by entering *(First Name) (Last Name)* in the Find What box and \2 \1 in the Replace With box. Word finds occurrences of the name and inverts the order so that the last name (item 2) comes first.

To display the Replace tab of the Find And Replace dialog box

→ On the **Home** tab, in the **Editing** group, click **Replace**.

→ Press **Ctrl+H**.

To search and replace by using wildcard characters

1. Display the **Replace** tab of the **Find and Replace** dialog box.

2. If the **Search Options** area isn't displayed, click **More**.

3. Select the **Use wildcards** check box.

4. In the **Find what** box, enter the wildcard expression for the text you want to find. Select wildcard characters from the **Special** menu or enter the wildcard character sequence yourself.

5. In the **Replace with** box, enter any replacement text or select an option from the **Special** menu.

6. Click **Find Next** to locate the first instance of the search term.

7. Click **Replace** or **Replace All** as appropriate to replace the search term.

Use special characters to find and replace text

To find and replace formatting marks, a character such as an em dash, or a field, you make selections from the Special menu in the Find And Replace dialog box. Special characters are represented by a character combination that begins with the caret symbol (^).

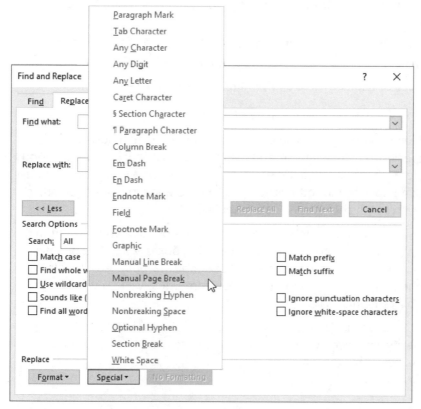

Insert character codes from the Special menu to find and replace special characters such as paragraph marks, notes, and dashes

In a document with extra paragraph characters, for example, you could search for two paragraph characters (^p^p) and replace the pair with one. If you wanted to search for any year between 2000 and 2007 and replace each year with 2017, you could enter 2^#^#^# (a 2 and three instances of the Any Digit option) in the Find What box and 2017 in the Replace With box.

Items on the Special menu vary depending on whether you are specifying values in the Find What box or the Replace With box. For example, you can choose *Clipboard Contents* as the value in the Replace With box to replace what you are searching for with the content saved on the Clipboard.

To search and replace by using special characters

1. Display the **Replace** tab of the **Find and Replace** dialog box. If necessary, click **More** to display the Search Options area.

2. In the **Find what** box, enter any text that you want to include in the search term.

3. Click the **Special** button, and then on the menu, click the special character you want to enter in the box. Repeat as necessary to enter multiple special characters.

4. In the **Replace with** box, enter any replacement text or special characters.

5. Click **Find Next** to locate the first instance of the search term.

6. Click **Replace** or **Replace All** as appropriate to replace the search term.

Find and replace formatting and styles

In the Find And Replace dialog box, you can use the Format menu to locate text formatted with a specific font, for example, and then replace that font with another. You can also search for formatting attributes such as font size or color, paragraph settings such as line spacing, specific tab settings, text in a specific language, or text or other document elements to which a specific style is applied.

The options on the Format menu open dialog boxes like those that you open from the Home tab to apply or modify formatting. In those dialog boxes, you select or enter settings for the format you want to search for (for example, 12-point Arial font with italic applied), and then specify settings for the new formatting you want to apply (14-point Calibri with a red font color).

When you select Style on the Format menu, you can use options in the Find Style dialog box to specify a style you want to locate and a style with which you want to replace that style.

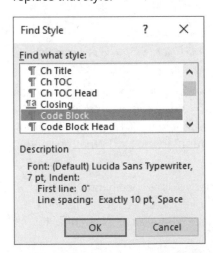

In the Description area, you can verify the attributes of the style you're searching for

When you use these find-and-replace operations to find and replace only formatting or styles (leaving the related text unchanged), you don't enter any text or other values in the Find What and Replace With boxes. However, you can search for and replace text by using the formatting or style applied to that text. For example, you could search for instances of the text *Office 2013* that have the Version Number style applied and replace those instances with the text *Office 2016*.

To find and replace formatting

1. Display the **Replace** tab of the **Find and Replace** dialog box. If necessary, click **More** to display the Search Options area.

2. Click in the **Find what** box, and then click **Format**. On the **Format** menu, click the type of formatting you want to find. In the dialog box that opens, specify the formatting, and then click **OK**.

3. Click in the **Replace with** box. On the **Format** menu, click the command for the type of formatting you need. In the dialog box that opens, specify the formatting you want to substitute, and then click **OK**.

4. Click **Find Next** to locate the first instance of the formatting.

5. Click **Replace** or **Replace All** as appropriate to substitute the new formatting.

To find and replace styles

1. Display the **Replace** tab of the **Find and Replace** dialog box. If necessary, click **More** to display the Search Options area.

2. Click in the **Find what** box, and then click **Format**.

3. On the **Format** menu, click **Style**.

4. In the **Find Style** dialog box, click the style you want to find, and then click **OK**.

5. Click in the **Replace with** box.

6. On the **Format** menu, click **Style**.

7. In the **Replace Style** dialog box, click the style you want to substitute, and then click **OK**.

8. Click **Find Next** to locate the first instance of the style.

9. Click **Replace** or **Replace All** as appropriate to substitute the new style.

To find and replace text by using formatting or styles

1. Display the **Replace** tab of the **Find and Replace** dialog box. If necessary, click **More** to display the Search Options area.

2. Click in the **Find what** box, enter the text you want to find, and then click **Format**.

2

3. On the **Format** menu, click the command for the type of formatting applied to the text or click **Style** to search for text with a specific style applied.

4. In the dialog box that opens, specify the formatting or style, and then click **OK**.

5. In the **Replace with** box, enter the text you want to substitute.

6. Click **Find Next** to locate the first instance of the text.

7. Click **Replace** or **Replace All** as appropriate to substitute the new style.

Set advanced page layout options

The layout of a Word document involves elements such as margins, page size, page orientation, and columns. Other elements of a document's layout include headers and footers, borders, and page and section breaks. You control the layout of a Word document by applying options from the Layout tab and other command groups on the ribbon. For more advanced layout options, you often work in the Page Setup dialog box and in dialog boxes with settings that affect layout elements such as line numbers and hyphens.

Work with document sections

By creating sections within a document, you can apply different page layout options to each section. For example, in a document that includes wide tables and illustrations in addition to text, the text sections could use the default Portrait orientation, and you could then create sections in which to include the tables and illustrations and set the page orientation for those sections to Landscape. You can change the settings for the following elements within a document section:

- **Headers and footers** Text and page numbering in the headers or footers can differ between sections.

- **Footnotes** Note numbers can restart within a section (or notes can be numbered consecutively throughout a document).

- **Margins** Page margins can vary from section to section.

- **Page orientation** One section can use Landscape orientation, and another can use the Portrait setting.

- **Paper size** One section can use letter size while another section uses legal.

- **Columns** The number of columns can vary in different document sections.

Many of the dialog boxes you use to specify page layout options (the Page Setup dialog box, for example) include the Apply To list. The items in this list (This Section, This Point Forward, and Whole Document) control the scope of the layout settings and options you select.

When you insert a section break, you can choose from four types:

- **Next Page** Starts the new section on the next page.
- **Continuous** Starts the new section on the same page as the current section. You can, for example, have sections with a different number of columns on the same page.
- **Even Page** Starts the new section on the next even-numbered page. If the following page is an odd-numbered page, that page is left blank.
- **Odd Page** Starts the new section on the next odd-numbered page. If the following page is an even-numbered page, that page is left blank.

Tip Word inserts section breaks automatically when you apply certain formatting to selected text. For example, if you select one or more paragraphs on a page and then format those paragraphs so that they appear in two or three columns, Word inserts continuous section breaks before and after the selected text.

The Layout tab of the Page Setup dialog box contains settings related to sections. You can display the Layout page by double-clicking the marker for a section break.

The Section Start area of the Layout tab shows what type of section break you are working with. When the cursor is in the section that follows a section break, you can use the Section Start list to change the type of the section break (from Continuous to Next Page, for example). On the Layout tab, you can also select an option for using different headers and footers on odd and even pages within a section and using a different header on the first page of a section. When you define a header or a footer for a section, you can use the Link To Previous command (in the Navigation group on the Header & Footer Design tool tab) to break the link between the header and footer in the previous section and create a new header or footer for the current section.

IMPORTANT If you delete a section break, any section formatting applied to the content or pages in that section reverts to the formatting specified for the section that follows the deleted section.

To insert a section break

1. Click in the document where you want to start the new section.
2. On the **Layout** tab, in the **Page Setup** group, click **Breaks**, and then click the type of section break you want to insert: **Next Page**, **Continuous**, **Even Page**, or **Odd Page**.

To display formatting marks

→ On the **Home** tab, in the **Paragraph** group, click the **Show/Hide** button.

→ Press **Ctrl+*** (**Ctrl+Shift+8**).

To delete a section break

1. Display formatting marks.
2. Select the section break you want to delete, and then press **Delete**.

To change the type of a section

1. Place the cursor in the section you want to change.
2. On the **Layout** tab, in the **Page Setup** group, click the dialog box launcher.
3. On the **Layout** tab of the **Page Setup** dialog box, in the **Section start** list, select the section type you want. Then click **OK**.

Set up pages

The Page Setup group on the Layout tab provides built-in commands that you can use to set margins, page orientation, page size, and the number of columns on the page—for example, narrow or wide margins, legal and other paper sizes, and two or three columns. To fine-tune the built-in settings and work with more advanced options for setting up a page, you can open the Page Setup dialog box.

On the Margins tab of the dialog box, the settings in the Margins area determine the width of a document's margins along its boundaries. Increasing the value in the Gutter box (which is 0 inches by default) creates space that can be used to bind facing pages, as in a bound book or a report.

Settings in the Multiple Pages list change margin and gutter options

The setting specified in the Pages area, in the Multiple Pages list, affects which margins you set. The following options are available:

- **Normal** With this setting, you set margins for Top, Bottom, Left, and Right. You can specify the measurement for a gutter and position the gutter at the left or the top of the document. (The Preview area in the dialog box shows how settings affect the document's layout.)

- **Mirror margins** This setting applies to a document you are printing on both sides of a sheet of paper. With this setting, you set margins for Top, Bottom, Inside, and Outside. You can set a gutter to appear between pages (where the pages might be bound).

- **2 pages per sheet** The margin settings for this option are Outside, Inside, Left, and Right. You can also set a gutter along the top and bottom of the page.

- **Book fold** The settings for Book Fold are Top, Bottom, Inside, and Outside. You can specify a gutter between facing pages.

The Paper tab of the Page Setup dialog box provides a list that includes the same paper sizes that are in the Size menu on the ribbon (in the Page Setup group on the Layout tab), but it also includes the Custom Size option. By using this option, you can specify the exact width and height of the page. For example, a book might use a page size of 7 inches by 9 inches instead of the standard letter-size page. In a document in which you have defined more than one section, you can specify a different paper source (a printer tray) for each section if you need to.

> **See Also** For information about working with settings on the Layout tab of the Page Setup dialog box, see "Work with document sections" earlier in this topic.

The Page Setup group on the Layout tab also provides options for using columns in a document's layout, in addition to options for controlling hyphenation and line numbers.

The Columns dialog box provides five preset choices for columns (the same set as on the Column menu in the Page Setup group) and a list in which you can specify up to 13 columns for a page. You can adjust the spacing between columns and the column width (by default, multiple columns are all the same width), and you can select an option to display a line between columns.

Use the Breaks menu on the ribbon to insert manual page breaks, column breaks, and section breaks. The Text Wrapping command on the Breaks menu inserts additional space to keep text and objects more distinct.

2

The Line Numbers command inserts line numbers along the left margin of a document. Line numbers are often used in legal documents for ease of reference. You can select an option to display line numbers continuously through a document or to start line numbering with each new page or section. You can also turn off line numbering for a specific paragraph and set line-numbering options such as the distance between line numbers and text.

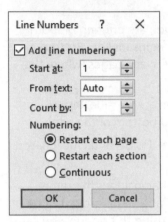

You can display line numbers that use a specific interval by changing the value in the Count By list

Hyphenation also affects the appearance of a page. Word by default does not hyphenate a document. If you choose to have Word hyphenate a document automatically, you can set an option to limit the number of consecutive hyphens. If you hyphenate a document manually, Word displays a dialog box in which you can confirm the hyphenation Word suggests or reposition a hyphen within a word.

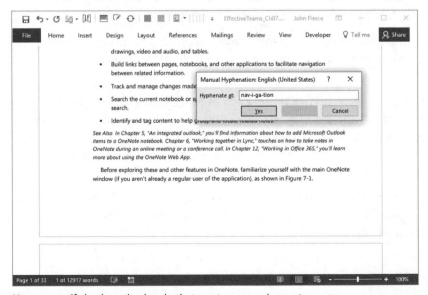

You can specify hyphenation breaks that meet your requirements

To set custom margins

1. On the **Layout** tab, in the **Page Setup** group, click **Margins**, and then click **Custom Margins** to display the Margins tab of the Page Setup dialog box.

2. In the **Pages** area, in the **Multiple pages** list, click the configuration you want to apply to the document: **Normal**, **Mirror margins**, **2 pages per sheet**, or **Book fold**.

3. In the **Margins** area, enter the values for margins and a gutter if the page layout requires one.

4. In the **Apply to** list, click an option for the scope of these settings: **This section**, **This point forward**, or **Whole document**.

> **IMPORTANT** The Apply To list includes the This Section option only if the document has multiple sections.

5. Click **OK**.

To set a custom paper size

1. On the **Layout** tab, in the **Page Setup** group, click **Size**, and then click **More Paper Sizes**.

2. On the **Paper** tab of the **Page Setup** dialog box, in the **Paper size** list, click **Custom size**.

3. In the **Width** and **Height** boxes, enter the dimensions for the page size.

4. In the **Apply to** list, click an option for the scope of these settings: **This section**, **This point forward**, or **Whole document**.

> **IMPORTANT** The Apply To list includes the This Section option only if the document has multiple sections.

5. Click **OK**.

To set up custom columns

1. On the **Layout** tab, in the **Page Setup** group, click **Columns**, and then click **More Columns**.

2. In the **Columns** dialog box, select a preset number or layout of columns, or use the **Number of columns** box to specify the number of columns you want to create.

3. If you want to insert a line between each column, select the **Line between** check box.

4. In the **Width and spacing** area, specify settings for the width and spacing for a column or columns, or keep **Equal column width** selected.

5. In the **Apply to** list, click an option for the scope of these settings: **This section**, **This point forward**, or **Whole document**.

> IMPORTANT The Apply To list includes the This Section option only if the document has multiple sections.

6. If you select **This point forward**, select the **Start new column** check box to insert a new column or columns where you are currently working in the document.

7. Click **OK**.

To assign line numbers

→ On the **Layout** tab, in the **Page Setup** group, click **Line Numbers**, and then click a preset option: **None**, **Continuous**, **Restart Each Page**, **Restart Each Section**, or **Suppress for Current Paragraph**.

Or

1. On the **Layout** tab, in the **Page Setup** group, click **Line Numbers**, and then click **Line Numbering Options**.

2. On the **Layout** tab of the **Page Setup** dialog box, click the **Line Numbers** button.

3. In the **Line Numbers** dialog box, select the **Add line numbering** check box.

4. In the **Start at** list, click the beginning line number.

5. In the **From text** list, specify the distance the line number will appear from the left margin of the text, or keep the default setting of **Auto**.

6. In the **Count by** list, specify the increment by which line numbers are displayed.

7. In the **Numbering** area, select the option for how line numbers should be displayed: **Restart each page**, **Restart each section**, or **Continuous**.

8. Click **OK** in the **Line Numbers** dialog box, and then click **OK** in the **Page Setup** dialog box.

To automatically hyphenate a document

1. On the **Layout** tab, in the **Page Setup** group, click **Hyphenation**, and then click **Hyphenation Options**.

2. In the **Hyphenation** dialog box, select the **Automatically hyphenate document** check box.

3. In the **Limit consecutive hyphens to** box, enter or select the maximum number of consecutive hyphenated lines that a paragraph can contain.

4. Click **OK**.

To manually hyphenate a word

1. In the document, select the word you want to hyphenate.
2. On the **Layout** tab, in the **Page Setup** group, click **Hyphenation**, and then click **Manual**.
3. In the **Manual Hyphenation** dialog box, accept the hyphenation suggested by Word or insert a hyphen where you want to break the word.

Adjust paragraph spacing and indentation

Use the options in the Paragraph group on the Layout tab to change the indentation of text and the spacing before and after paragraphs. The dialog box launcher in the Paragraph group opens the Paragraph dialog box with the Indents And Spacing page displayed.

Tip You can specify line spacing and indention settings when you create a paragraph style. For more information, see "Create paragraph and character styles" in "Objective 2.2: Create styles."

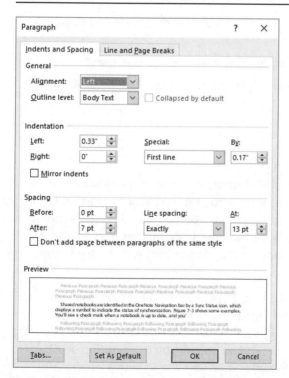

Options in the Spacing area control spacing between paragraphs and between lines of text

By using the options in the Paragraph dialog box, you can refine indentation and settings for line spacing. In the Indentation area, you select Mirror Indents if you are setting up a document to print on both sides of a sheet. The Special list is used to create paragraphs in which the first line is indented more than other lines or to create a hanging indent, in which the first line is indented less. A hanging indent is often used to create bulleted lists.

In the Spacing area, you can select a standard setting from the Line Spacing list (Single, Double, or 1.5) or use the At Least or Exactly option. With both of these options, you specify a value for line spacing in the At list. With the At Least option, Word uses either this value or the font size to fit the largest font or graphic in a line. The Exactly option applies the height you specify regardless of content.

To adjust paragraph specifications

1. On the **Layout** tab, in the **Paragraph** group, click the dialog box launcher.

2. In the **Paragraph** dialog box, in the **Indentation** area, do either of the following:

   - Set indentation for the left and right sides of the page.

   - Select **Mirror indents**, and then specify values for the inside and outside borders of the page.

3. In the **Spacing** area, specify spacing for before and after a paragraph.

4. In the **Line Spacing** list, select a standard setting, or select **Exactly** or **At Least** and then specify the line spacing you want to use.

5. Click **OK**.

Arrange objects on pages

When you lay out a document that contains illustrations, images, charts, or other objects, you can use the options in the Arrange group on the Layout tab to position the objects and specify how text wraps around them. You can also change the order of objects and specify how objects are aligned within the document. You are likely to need to arrange objects when you are producing documents such as newsletters, magazines, and illustrated reports.

Text and objects appear on different "layers" in a document. You can position an object in line with a document's text—on the same layer—which means that the object can be positioned only within a single paragraph, with no text wrapping around the object. When you wrap text around an object, you can position an object anywhere within the document, even behind text, as you would with a watermark.

Tip Use Bring Forward, Send Backward, and related commands to change the position of an object in relation to other objects and to text.

Word provides several preset position and wrapping options. Use the options in the Position gallery in the Arrange group to orient the object on the page, either in line with the text or positioned at the top, middle, or bottom along either margin or centered within the text at the top, middle, or bottom of the page. Options on the Wrap Text menu adjust how the object and text appear together. The Tight option, for example, causes the text to wrap to reflect the object's shape and dimensions. The Square option positions text roughly equally along each side of an object.

You can drag an object to change its position or use the Layout dialog box to work with a variety of options that effect the object's position, size, and relationship to text. You can open the Layout dialog box by clicking More Layout Options at the bottom of the Position or Wrap Text menu.

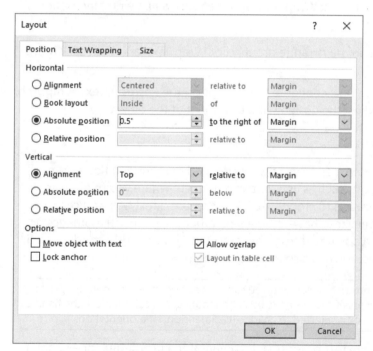

Use the list settings to orient objects with the margin, page, column, or other options

When an object is not positioned in line with text, use the options and settings in the Horizontal and Vertical areas on the Position tab of the Layout dialog box to control the position of the object in relation to the margin, page, column, paragraph, or line. You can position the object at the distance you specify (Absolute Position) or use a relative position—in case the document's margin changes, for example. Other options on the Position tab of the Layout dialog box can be used to anchor the object on the page or allow the object to move when text is inserted or deleted.

In addition to the preset wrapping options, the Text Wrapping tab of the Layout dialog box provides options for specifying whether text wraps on only a single side of an object or on the side with the most space (Largest Only). You can also specify values for the distance the text remains from the object along the top, bottom, and sides.

The Size tab of the Layout dialog box provides settings you use to precisely control the height, width, rotation, and scale of an object.

To set the position and text wrapping of a selected object on a page

1. On the **Layout** tab, in the **Arrange** group, click **Position**, and then select an option to position the object on the page.

2. In the **Arrange** group, click **Wrap Text**, and then click a text wrapping option.

Or

1. On the **Layout** tab, in the **Arrange** group, click **Wrap Text**, and then click **More Layout Options**.

2. In the **Layout** dialog box, configure the settings on the **Position**, **Text Wrapping**, and **Size** tabs to adjust the position and alignment of the object.

Link text boxes

In most Word documents, text appears between defined margins and flows from page to page. In documents such as newsletters or reports, where you might want to place text in a specific location to emphasize it, you can use a text box. You can work with text boxes in ways similar to how you manage other objects (such as images or shapes) that you add to a document from the Insert tab. You can add a border or a fill to a text box, for example. You can also rotate a text box.

Tip When you add a text box to a document, you can choose one of several built-in text box styles or draw a text box yourself to define the box's boundaries. You can then use the handles that appear when the text box is selected to change its dimensions and orientation.

When you add two or more text boxes to a document (for a newsletter, for example), you can link text boxes to facilitate the flow and editing of the text that the text boxes contain. When text boxes are linked, any text that does not fit within the boundaries of the first text box flows automatically to the linked text box. If you shorten or lengthen the text in linked text boxes, the text reflows to reflect the change.

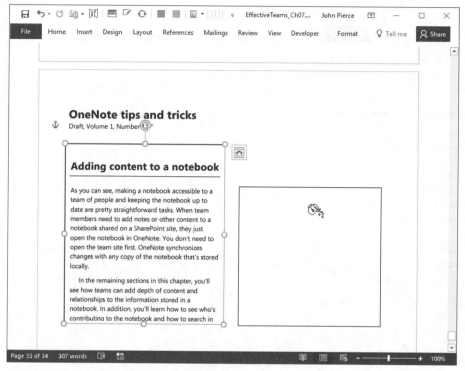

Word displays the cursor as a cup spilling letters when you link text boxes

---

IMPORTANT You can link only to an empty text box. Word displays an error message if you try to create a link to a text box that already contains text.

Word displays visual hints during the steps you follow to link text boxes. The mouse pointer changes during this process to resemble first an upright cup (when you select the first text box, which already contains text) and then a cup spilling letters, which is your clue that when you select the second text box (which must be empty), text will flow to it from the first. (Linked text boxes are not identified by icons or other visual aids.)

To link text boxes

1. Select the text box that you want to link from.
2. On the **Format** tool tab, in the **Text** group, click **Create Link**.
3. Click the text box you want to link to.

To break the link between text boxes

1. Select the linked text box.
2. On the **Format** tool tab, in the **Text** group, click **Break Link**.

Set paragraph pagination options

The Line And Page Breaks tab of the Paragraph dialog box provides options that you can use to control various aspects of page layout.

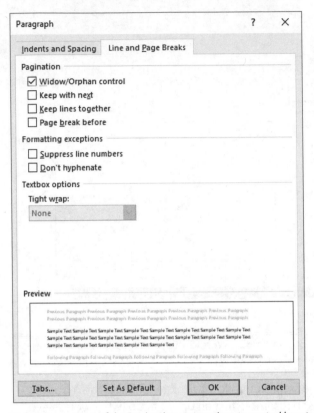

Select one or more of the Pagination area options to control how text breaks across a page

In the Pagination group, use the following settings to manage pagination:

- **Widow/Orphan control** A *widow* is a single line of text that appears at the bottom of a page, and an *orphan* is a single line that appears at the top of a page. Selecting this option controls widows and orphans by preventing single lines of text at either the start or the end of a page.

- **Keep with next** This option keeps the lines of text you select together with the paragraph that follows them. You might apply this setting to a heading and the paragraph that follows it so that the heading does not stand alone on the page.

- **Keep lines together** When you want to keep lines of text together on a page (the stanza of a poem or a quotation, for example), select that text and then set this option.

- **Page break before** Select this option to insert a page break before selected text.

In the Formatting Exceptions area of the Line And Page Breaks tab, there are two options:

- **Suppress line numbers** Use this option to turn off the display of line numbers for the active paragraph.

- **Don't hyphenate** Use this option to turn off hyphenation in the active paragraph.

The Textbox Options area of the dialog box provides settings for controlling whether the text that wraps a text box is tightly wrapped. You can apply one of the following settings to the active paragraph: None, All, First and Last Lines, First Line Only, and Last Line Only.

To set paragraph pagination options

1. On the **Layout** tab, in the **Paragraph** group, click the dialog box launcher.

2. On the **Line and Page Breaks** tab of the **Paragraph** dialog box, do any of the following:

   - In the **Pagination** area, select any of the **Widow/Orphan control**, **Keep with next**, **Keep lines together**, and **Page break before** check boxes.

   - In the **Formatting exceptions** area, select either or both of the **Suppress line numbers** and **Don't hyphenate** check boxes.

   - In the **Textbox options** area, if the **Tight wrap** list is active, select an option for how to wrap text around the selected text box.

3. Click **OK** to apply the settings.

Resolve style conflicts

Copying and pasting text and other content is a standard operation when you work with more than one document. If the styles in the documents you are working with have the same definitions, the text and other content will retain the formatting from the source document. If the same styles in the source and destination documents have conflicting definitions, Word uses the style definition in the destination document by default.

When Word detects a conflict in styles, it displays a Paste Options button. You can click the button (or press Ctrl) to open a gallery of icons that provides options for how the content you are pasting should be formatted. You can use the destination formatting, use the source formatting, merge formatting, or keep only the text (so that the content is pasted using the default Normal style). If Live Preview is enabled, Word displays how each option affects the display of the pasted content when you point to the option's icon.

By selecting settings on the Advanced page of the Word Options dialog box, you can control how Word manages style conflicts when you paste content between multiple documents. The settings you work with are in the Cut, Copy, And Paste section.

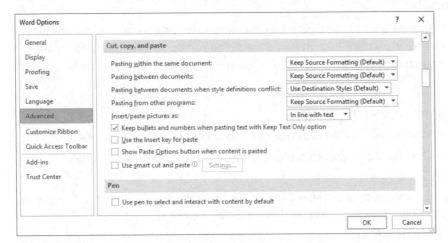

Configure options for cutting, copying, and pasting content

From the options in the Pasting Between Documents When Style Definitions Conflict list, select the setting that you want Word to use by default. The settings include the following:

- Use Destination Styles (the default setting)
- Keep Source Formatting
- Merge Formatting
- Keep Text Only

In the Word Options dialog box, click the Settings button next to the Use Smart Cut And Paste option to open the Settings dialog box. The Smart Style Behavior option in this dialog box also affects how Word manages style conflicts. When this option is selected, styles are handled consistently when the style in the document you are pasting from has the same name as a style in the document you are pasting to. The Paste options allow you to choose between keeping the formatting and matching the formatting of the destination document.

To resolve style conflicts when pasting content between documents

1. In the destination document, click the **Paste Options** button that Word displays when it detects a style conflict.

2. Point to the paste option icons, refer to the live preview to view how each option affects the content you are pasting, and then click the option you want to apply.

2

Objective 2.1 practice tasks

The practice file for these tasks is located in the **MOSWordExpert2016 \Objective2** practice file folder. The folder also contains a result file that you can use to check your work.

➤ Open the **WordExpert_2-1** document, and do the following:

❑ Use wildcards in the Find And Replace dialog box to locate instances of *Ms. Kim Akers* and *Miss Kim Akers*, and then replace those instances with <u>Kim Akers</u>.

❑ Use wildcards in the Find And Replace dialog box to locate words that end in <u>ful</u>.

❑ Use the *\n* wildcard character to replace the phrase *search online* with <u>online search</u>.

❑ Find instances of two consecutive paragraph marks and replace them with a single paragraph mark.

❑ Find instances of the Heading 1 style and replace it with the Heading 2 style.

❑ Find Dark Blue text and change its font color to Green.

❑ Insert a continuous section break before the heading for section 1 and another before the heading for section 2.

❑ Define custom margins for the new section, specifying 1.5 inches for the top and bottom margins.

❑ Select the second and third paragraphs in section 1 and arrange the text in three columns. Set the spacing between columns 1 and 2 to 0.75 inches.

❑ Select the text in the columns, and then set the line spacing to exactly 10 points.

❑ In section 2, resize the picture to be 4.45 inches high and 2.5 inches wide. Position it in the upper-right corner of the page, and then select the Tight text wrapping option.

❑ In section 3, link the text boxes. Delete or insert text in the first text box to observe how the text reflows.

➤ Open the **WordExpert_2-1_results** document. Compare the two documents to check your work. Then close the open documents.

Objective 2.2: Create styles

Every paragraph in a Word document is assigned a specific style. You can create an entire document that uses only the default Normal style and then format the text and other elements by adding bold or italic, increasing or decreasing font size, applying different fonts, and adding text effects. But even in a document that contains only one or two levels of headings and regular paragraphs of text, you need to do a lot of work to make elements of the same type consistent. Styles provide much more control and consistency in how the elements of a document appear, and after you apply styles to your document, you can change a style's properties once and Word updates the style throughout the document.

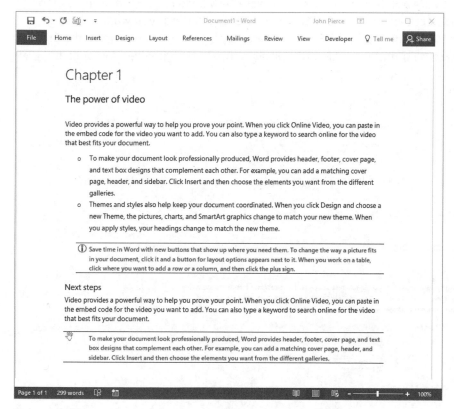

Styles maintain a consistent appearance throughout a document

---

Tip To easily check which style is applied to each paragraph in a document, switch to Draft or Outline view. (You might need to increase the width of the style area pane, which you can do in the Word Options dialog box, in the Display section of the Advanced page.) Word also highlights the style applied to the selected paragraph in the Styles gallery.

This section describes how to create styles and how to modify a style—either a style you create or one of the styles defined in Word by default.

Create paragraph and character styles

In creating a set of styles for a document or a template, you most often work with paragraph and character styles (styles you use to format words or single characters within a paragraph). Both paragraph and character styles include settings such as font, font size, and font color. Paragraph styles also include attributes for alignment, line spacing, and indentation and can include settings related to text effects, numbering, and other properties.

When you create a style, you work in the Create New Style From Formatting dialog box. If you select text and format it to reflect the style settings you want (by using options on the Home tab, in the Font and Paragraph groups, for example), the Create New Style From Formatting dialog box displays those settings when you open it.

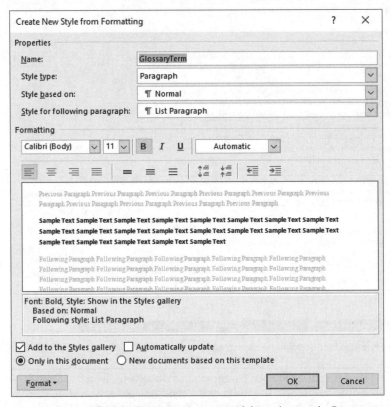

You can use the controls in the Formatting area and the options on the Format menu to further define style attributes

In the Properties area of the Create New Style From Formatting dialog box, you specify the style's name, the type of style you want to create, and which style the new style is based on. If you are creating a paragraph style, you can also specify the style Word applies automatically to a paragraph that follows the paragraph the new style is applied to. Use the fields in the Properties area as follows:

- **Name** Style names are case-sensitive (MyStyle and Mystyle would be considered distinct styles), and you cannot create a style that uses the name of a style built in to Word—for example, you cannot create a style named Normal (although you can modify built-in styles, as described in the next section).

- **Style type** The types of styles are paragraph, character, linked, table, and list. A linked style is a special case. When you select a linked style, Word applies the character formatting defined in a style (font color, for example, but not line spacing) or the style's full definition depending on what is selected in the document. When one or more words are selected, selecting a linked style applies the style's character formatting. Text that isn't selected is not changed and keeps the current paragraph formatting. If you select the paragraph or place the cursor within the paragraph, a linked style applies both the character and paragraph settings defined in the style.

  For a table style, you specify standard attributes such as font and paragraph settings, but you can also select settings for borders and shading and how many rows or columns (if any) are banded to display the same background. For a list style, you can select settings for different levels. For example, you can set the top level to be numbered 1, 2, 3, with a second level identified with a, b, c, and so on.

- **Style based on** Select a style whose properties you want to use as the basis for the new style. If you base a style on the built-in Normal style, for example, and then change the font for the Normal style from Calibri to Garamond, Word also changes the font for styles based on the Normal style to Garamond.

- **Style for following paragraph** Select the style for paragraphs that follow paragraphs that use this style. Word assigns that style when you insert a paragraph break by pressing Enter. For a heading style, for example, specify Normal or another body text style in this list.

In many cases, you can capture all the formatting details you need in a paragraph style—indentation, font size, line spacing, and other such details. Within a paragraph, you can format characters by using the controls in the Font group on the Home tab or by choosing options in the Font dialog box. For more control over character formatting, you can also create styles specifically for groups of characters and then apply those styles as you format the document.

2

When you select Character in the Style Type list in the Create New Style From Formatting dialog box, the options in the dialog box change so that they apply only to character styles.

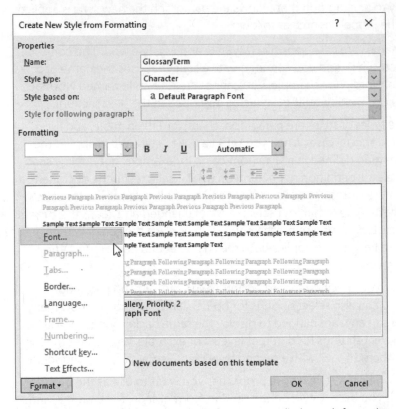

When you are creating a character style, the Format menu displays only formatting options relevant to character styles

In the Style Based On list, Word displays Default Paragraph Font. Open the Style Based On list, and then choose from among the built-in character styles if you want to use one of them as a starting point. In the Formatting area of the dialog box, only controls related to character formatting are available to define the style. The Format menu also restricts which formatting options you can apply to a character style.

To create a paragraph style

1. Display the **Styles** pane.

2. At the bottom of the **Styles** pane, click the **New Style** button.

3. In the **Create New Style from Formatting** dialog box, define the style's properties (name, type, and others), and then specify the font, font attributes, indentation, line spacing, and other settings that define the style.

4. For more detailed settings, click **Format**, choose the type of element you want to format, specify the settings you want in the relevant dialog box, and then click **OK**.

5. To save the new style in the current template, select **New documents based on this template**.

6. Click **OK** to create the style.

To create a character style

1. In the **Create New Style from Formatting** dialog box, select **Character** in the **Style type** list.

2. Use the controls in the **Formatting** area to define the attributes of the style.

3. For more detailed settings, click **Format**, choose the type of element you want to format, specify the settings you want in the relevant dialog box, and then click **OK**.

4. To save the new style in the current template, select **New documents based on this template**.

5. Click **OK** to create the style.

Modify styles

The basic settings that define a style include font properties (font, size, and color), formatting such as bold or italic, text alignment (centered, flush left, flush right, or justified), line spacing, spacing between paragraphs, and indentation. Style definitions can also include settings for character spacing, borders, and text effects such as shadows, text outlines, and fills. The styles you create and the styles defined by default in the standard Normal template are all defined by using attributes and settings such as these.

By changing these settings, you can modify a built-in style, a style you created, or a style that's defined in the template a document is based on. The Modify Style dialog box lists a style's properties in the preview area.

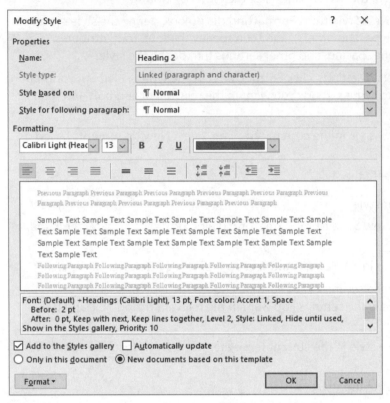

Select the New Documents option to save style changes in the template attached to the document

Many of a style's basic settings can be modified by using the controls in the Formatting area of the Modify Style dialog box. (These settings are roughly the same as the settings in the Font and Paragraph groups on the Home tab.) The Format button at the bottom of the dialog box opens a menu with commands that lead to dialog boxes that provide options to refine settings for basic elements, including font and paragraph settings, and also to define or update settings for borders, frames, list formats, and special text effects.

When you modify a style, be sure to review the check boxes and option buttons at the bottom of the Modify Style dialog box. Keep the Add To Styles Gallery option selected if you have renamed a style, for example, and want to add it to the Styles gallery on the Home tab. Select Automatically Update only if you want to automatically update a style's definition with formatting changes you make to text the style is applied to. Those changes are reflected in all instances of the style in a document.

If you want to make the changes to a style part of the style's definition in the associated template, select New Documents Based On This Template. Keep the option Only In This Document selected if that's the scope you're working with.

You can also modify an existing style by selecting text that uses the style and then formatting the text by using controls in the Font and Paragraph groups on the Home tab. When the text has the formatting you want for the style, right-click the style's name in the Styles gallery (or the Styles pane), and then click Update Style Name To Match Selection.

Tip In the Word Options dialog box, in the Editing section on the Advanced page, select Prompt To Update Style to have Word display a dialog box when you apply a style from the Styles gallery that includes updated formatting. In the dialog box, Word prompts you to update the style to include the recent changes or to reapply the formatting defined in the style.

To modify an existing style

1. In the **Styles** gallery or **Styles** pane, right-click the style, and then click **Modify**.

2. In the **Modify Style** dialog box, revise the style's properties by changing the font, specific font attributes, indentation, line spacing, and other settings.

3. For more detailed settings, click **Format**, choose the type of element you want to format, specify the settings you want in the relevant dialog box, and then click **OK**.

4. To save the changes to this style in the current template, select **New documents based on this template**.

5. Click **OK**.

Tip Applying styles by using keyboard shortcuts helps you format a document as you enter the document's text and other content. Word provides keyboard shortcuts for several of its built-in styles. You can assign your own keyboard shortcut to a style when you create it or when you modify the style's properties. In the Create New Style From Formatting dialog box or the Modify Style dialog box, you can open the Customize Keyboard dialog box from the Format menu.

Objective 2.2 practice tasks

The practice file for these tasks is located in the **MOSWordExpert2016
\Objective2** practice file folder. The folder also contains a result file that
you can use to check your work.

➤ Open the **WordExpert_2-2** document, and do the following:

❑ Modify the *Book Extract* style as follows:

  ○ Remove the hanging first line indent.

  ○ Change the font color to Light Blue.

  ○ Add top and bottom borders with a width of 1 pt.

❑ Create a paragraph style named <u>Author Bio</u>. Use 11 pt. Century
as the font, with an italic font style. Set the line spacing to exactly
12 pt. Set the spacing before the paragraph to 6 pt. and after the
paragraph to 12 pt.

❑ Create a paragraph style named <u>Back Matter Title</u>. Select *Author
Bio* as the style for the following paragraph. Use the Arial font set
to 14 pt. and bold. Assign the keyboard shortcut Ctrl+Alt+9 to the
style. (Use a different shortcut if that one is already assigned to
something.)

❑ Scroll to the end of the document and apply these styles to the
About the Author section.

❑ Create a character style named <u>Glossary Term</u>. Use Times New
Roman, 11 pt., bold italic, and the Dark Blue font color as the style's
attributes.

❑ Find instances of the *Emphasis* style in the document and replace
them with the *Glossary Term* style.

➤ Open the **WordExpert_2-2_results** document. Compare the two
documents to check your work. Then close the open documents.

Objective group 3
Create advanced references

The skills tested in this section of the Microsoft Office Specialist Expert exam for Microsoft Word 2016 relate to creating advanced references, including indexes and tables of contents. Specifically, the following objectives are associated with this set of skills:

3.1 Create and manage indexes

3.2 Create and manage reference tables

3.3 Manage forms, fields, and mail-merge operations

Business reports, academic papers, and book manuscripts are types of documents that often use references to help readers navigate the document or to meet a publisher's or an organization's requirements. Word includes features that help you create these references. Word also provides tools that you can use to produce bulk mailings or to capture specific document information by using fields.

This chapter guides you in studying ways of creating and managing indexes and reference tables and managing forms, fields, and mail-merge operations.

3

To complete the practice tasks in this chapter, you need the practice files contained in the **MOSWordExpert2016\Objective3** practice file folder. For more information, see "Download the practice files" in this book's introduction.

Objective 3.1: Create and manage indexes

Before you add an index to a document, you need to complete two general steps: mark index entries (by inserting index fields) and set options for how Word generates the index. Word uses the entries and the options you specify to create the index, assigning page numbers to the entries based on their location in the document.

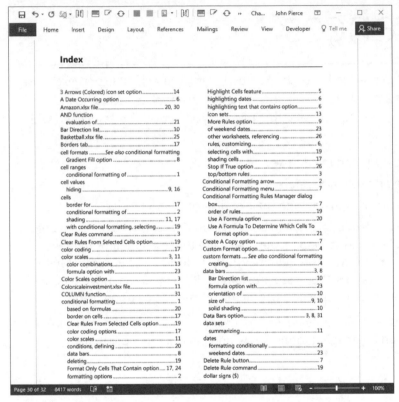

An example of a completed index, with main entries and indented subentries

You can use several approaches to mark index entries:

- Select the text you want to use as an entry.

- Add an entry of your own at the location where you want the index marker.

- Compile terms in a separate file, and have Word insert index markers based on the terms in the file.

An index entry must define at least one level, the main entry. Index entries can also include subentries and cross-references to other entries in the index. Entries can refer to a specific page or to a range of pages. For example, a main entry of *macros* might include subentries such as *recording*, *editing*, and *assigning to a button*. The page reference for the main entry might span several pages, with subentries covered on a single page or a span of fewer pages.

Mark index entries

When you insert entries manually by selecting or entering text, you work in the Mark Index Entry dialog box. If text is selected when you open the Mark Index Entry dialog box, that text is displayed in the Main Entry box. You can keep the Mark Index Entry dialog box open as you work on a document. Text that is selected when you click the dialog box to make it active replaces any text currently in the Main Entry box. You don't need to select text to create a main entry, however. You can define a main entry yourself by clicking where you want an index reference placed in the document and then entering the text in the Main Entry box.

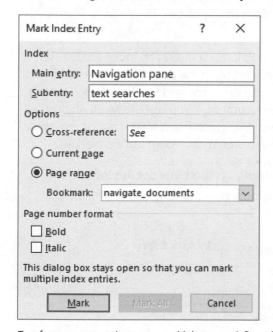

To reference content that spans multiple pages, define a bookmark and point the index entry to the bookmark

Tip You can apply formatting such as bold, italic, and underline to the text in the Main Entry, Subentry, and Cross-Reference boxes by selecting the text and then using the formatting keyboard shortcuts. For example, you might need to italicize the title of a book or journal or choose to display in bold terms that also appear in a glossary. The formatting you apply by using the formatting keyboard shortcuts does not override settings for index styles defined in the template attached to the document.

Subentries for a main entry must be entered manually. You can also create a third-level entry within the subentry or create a cross-reference (such as a *See* reference) to other index entries as needed.

Word defines index entries within hidden index fields. An index field is identified by the characters *XE*. Curly braces enclose the index field tag and text.

Tip If index fields are not displayed in your document, display hidden formatting marks.

Here is an example of the information that an index field might contain:

{ XE "formatting:characters: font" \t See also styles" }

An entry that spans a range of pages is associated with a bookmark that you define in the document. The bookmark is associated with the content that you want the index entry to refer to. The bookmark does not identify specific page numbers itself. The indexing feature in Word assigns page numbers to the bookmarked range when you generate the index.

The Mark All button in the Mark Index Entry dialog box inserts an index field at the first occurrence of the main entry in each paragraph of the document. For example, if the main entry is *styles*, clicking Mark All inserts an index field for the first occurrence of the word *styles* in each paragraph of the document. If you use the Mark All button, keep in mind that Word distinguishes between uppercase and lowercase occurrences of a term—in the previous example, occurrences of *Styles* would not be marked.

To display index entries and hidden formatting symbols in a document

➜ On the **Home** tab, in the **Paragraph** group, click **Show/Hide ¶**.

To open the Mark Index Entry dialog box

➜ On the **References** tab, in the **Index** group, click **Mark Entry**.

➜ Press **Alt+Shift+X**.

To mark index entries

1. Open the **Mark Index Entry** dialog box.

2. In the document, do either of the following:

   - Select the text for which you want to create a main index entry, and then click the **Mark Index Entry** dialog box to make it active.

   - Click where you want an index marker to be in the document, and then in the **Mark Index Entry** dialog box, enter the text for the entry in the **Main Entry** box.

3. If you want to define a second-level index term, enter the term in the **Subentry** box. If you want to define a third-level entry, add a colon to the end of the sub-entry, and then enter the third-level term.

4. In the **Options** area, do one of the following:

   - Click **Cross-reference**, and then enter the text for the reference.
   - Click **Current page**.
   - Click **Page range**, and then select the bookmark for the range of pages the entry is related to.

   > **See Also** For information about bookmarking page ranges, see the next procedure.

5. In the **Page number format** area, if you want Word to apply specific formatting to the page number, select the **Bold** or **Italic** check box.

6. Do either of the following:

   - To insert a single index entry in the current location, click **Mark.**
   - To insert an index entry for the first instance of the term in each paragraph of the document, click **Mark All**.

To create a bookmark that defines a page range

1. Select the paragraphs you want to include in the page range.

2. On the **Insert** tab, in the **Links** group, click **Bookmark**.

3. In the **Bookmark** dialog box, enter a name for the bookmark, and then click **Add**.

Insert index entries from a file

You can create an index by maintaining a file that contains main entries in a separate document (also referred to as an *automark file* or a *concordance file*) that Word uses to mark entries in the document being indexed. The automark file can be saved as a Word document or in other formats, such as a text (.txt) file. Each entry is set up as a separate paragraph. Word then searches for each term or phrase in the automark file and inserts a corresponding index field for the first instance of the term or phrase it finds in each paragraph of the document.

For more flexibility, you can set up the list in a two-column table, with the terms you want to search for in the left column and the corresponding index entries in the right column. By using two columns, you can collect terms such as *format*, *formatting*, and *formatted* under the same main entry—list the terms separately in the table's left column and enter the same main entry in the table's right column.

3

The entries in an automark file are case-sensitive. For example, if the automark file includes the term *text effects*, Word won't insert an index field for an instance of *Text effects* when it indexes the document.

To create an automark file

1. In a blank document, do one of the following:

   - Enter the index terms in individual paragraphs.

   - Create a two-column table. Enter terms that you want Word to index in the first column, and the index tags you want to associate with each term in the second column.

2. Save the file.

To mark index entries by using an automark file

1. On the **References** tab, in the **Index** group, click **Insert Index**.

2. In the **Index** dialog box, click **AutoMark**.

3. In the **Open Index AutoMark File** dialog box, browse to and select the automark file, and then click **Open**.

Create and update indexes

After you mark index entries, you use the options in the Index dialog box to specify the index's design and other options for the appearance of the index.

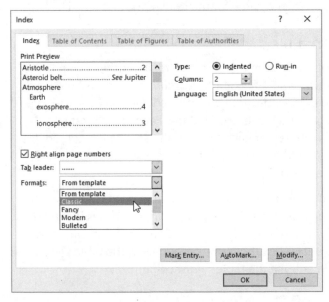

Choose a preset index format from the Formats list

Word supports two index formats: indented and run-in. By default, both formats appear in a two-column layout and are wrapped to fit the width of the columns. In an indented index, the entries are listed in this format:

Styles
   applying, 211
   creating, 209
   updating in template, 212

In a run-in index, an entry would appear as follows:

Styles: applying, 211; creating, 209; updating
   in template, 212

A run-in index saves space, which makes it a good choice if you have only a limited number of pages for the index. When you select an option for the type of index, Word displays an example in the Print Preview area of the Index dialog box.

You can change the number of columns (from 1 through 4) or set the Columns box to Auto (in which case the index uses the same number of columns as defined in the document). If you are using an indented index, you can change the alignment of page numbers. Word previews this format when you select the option, and you can then select the type of tab leader you want to include (or select None from this list). The Formats list provides several options for styling the fonts, line spacing, and other formats Word applies to the index entries when you generate the index.

Tip If From Template is selected in the Formats list, you can modify the styles for index levels. Click Modify in the Index dialog box. In the Style dialog box, select an index level, and then click Modify to open the Modify Style dialog box and make changes to the formatting attributes for that index level. For more information about modifying styles, see "Objective 2.2: Create styles."

If you need to edit an index entry, you should edit the specific index field and not the index that Word generates. By editing the entry, you ensure that corrections are included if you generate the index again. Locate the field in the document, and then edit and format the text enclosed in quotation marks within the curly braces that define the field.

After you make changes to index markers, you can easily update the index in place.

Tip When editing index entries, you can move between fields by using the search features on the Find and Go To tabs of the Find And Replace dialog box. To locate fields from the Find tab, click Field in the Special list. To locate fields from the Go To tab, click Field in the Go To What list.

3

To specify index formatting options and generate the index

1. In the document, click where you want to insert the index.

2. On the **References** tab, in the **Index** group, click **Insert Index**.

3. In the **Index** dialog box, set the following options, and then click **OK**:

   - In the **Type** area, click **Indented** or **Run-in**.

   - In the **Columns** box, enter or select the number of columns you want to arrange the index entries in.

   - If you are using a language other than the default language on your system, choose a language.

   - If you are using an indented index, select the **Right align page numbers** check box, and then select the style of tab leader you want to use.

   - Select a format for the index, or keep **From template** selected.

To edit index entries

1. In the document, display index entries and hidden formatting symbols.

2. Locate the index entry you want to edit, and edit the text within the index tag.

To delete index entries

1. In the document, display index entries and hidden formatting symbols.

2. Locate the index entry you want to delete.

3. Select the entire field (including the curly braces), and then press the **Delete** key.

To update an index

→ Click anywhere in the index, and then, on the **References** tab, in the **Index** group, click **Update Index**.

→ Right-click the index, and then click **Update Field**.

Objective 3.1 practice tasks

The practice files for these tasks are located in the **MOSWordExpert2016 \Objective3** practice file folder. The folder also contains result files that you can use to check your work.

➤ Open the **WordExpert_3-1a** document and do the following:

❑ Define a bookmark that starts with the section heading "Customizing settings for existing styles" and includes the whole section. Name the bookmark <u>customizing</u>.

❑ Work through the file, and add index entries for the following terms:

Create New Style From Formatting dialog box

Format menu

formatting

Home tab

Modify Style dialog box

Paragraph group

Style Based On list

styles

Styles gallery

template

❑ After the heading "Customizing settings for existing styles," insert a main entry for *styles* and a subentry for *modifying*. Use the bookmark named *customizing* to indicate the page range.

❑ After the heading "Create a character style," insert a main entry for *styles* and a subentry for *character style*.

❑ Generate a run-in index, placing the index at the end of the document.

❑ Find the entries for *formatting*, and edit the entries so that they read *formatting text*.

❑ Update the index to reflect your changes.

➤ Save the **WordExpert_3-1a** document.

➤ Open the **WordExpert_3-1a_results** document. Compare the two documents to check your work. (The number of entries and their placement in your document might differ from those shown in the result file.) When you are done, close the open documents.

➤ Open the **WordExpert_3-1b** document and do the following:

   ❑ In the blank document, create an automark file listing the same terms you used earlier, pressing Enter after each term.

➤ Save the **WordExpert_3-1b** document.

➤ Open the **WordExpert_3-1b_results** document. Compare the two documents to check your work. Then close the open documents.

➤ Open the **WordExpert_3-1c** document and do the following:

   ❑ Insert index entries by referencing the **WordExpert_3-1b** automark file.

   ❑ Generate an indented index, placing it at the end of the document.

➤ Save the **WordExpert_3-1c** document.

➤ Open the **WordExpert_3-1c_results** document. Compare the two documents to check your work. Then close the open documents.

Objective 3.2: Create and manage references

Word 2016 provides commands and options for creating and managing references such as tables of contents, captions, and tables of figures. This section describes how to customize a table of contents, manage captions for various types of objects (such as figures, tables, and charts), and to insert and update a table of figures.

Customize a table of contents

Word can use its built-in heading styles and other styles you specify to create a table of contents. When you build a table of contents from styles, you can update the table of contents by editing the headings in the body of the document and then regenerating the table of contents. You don't need to edit the headings in both locations. If styles are used in a document, you can insert a table of contents that follows one of two built-in styles or build a table of contents from scratch.

><><><><><><><><><><><><><><><><><><><><><><><><><><><><><><><><><><><><><><><><><><><><><

Exam Strategy Exam 77-726, "Word 2016 Expert: Creating Documents for Effective Communication," requires that you demonstrate the ability to customize a table of contents. Creating a table of contents that uses a built-in style and updating or deleting a table of contents are part of the objective domain for Exam 77-725, "Word 2016: Core Document Creation, Collaboration and Communication."

><><><><><><><><><><><><><><><><><><><><><><><><><><><><><><><><><><><><><><><><><><><><><

3

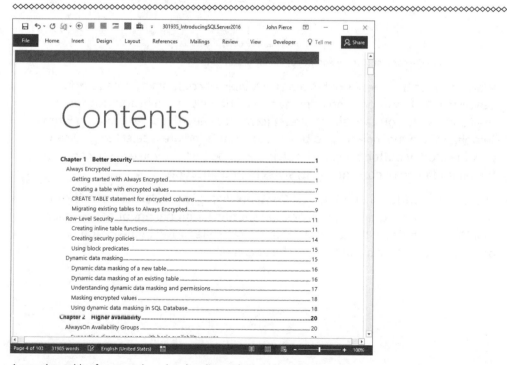

A complete table of contents based on heading styles in a document

You customize a table of contents from the Table Of Contents dialog box, which provides formatting options and a set of options for which levels of headings Word includes in the table of contents.

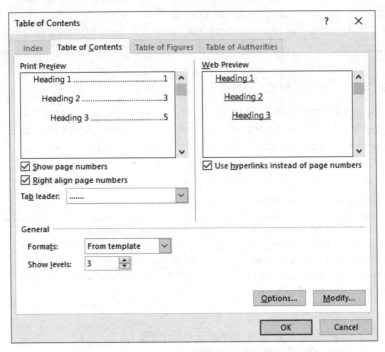

You can modify the content and appearance of a table of contents

Word includes three levels of headings in a table of contents by default. You can display as few as one and as many as nine of the built-in heading styles. In the Formats list, you can select a preset format or keep the default setting From Template. As in the Index dialog box, when From Template is selected, you can click the Modify button to open the Style dialog box, where you can select one of the built-in table of contents (TOC) styles for modification.

The Options button in the Table Of Contents dialog box opens a dialog box in which you can designate other styles and specify additional options for elements that Word includes in the table of contents. The styles listed in the dialog box depend on the template applied to the document.

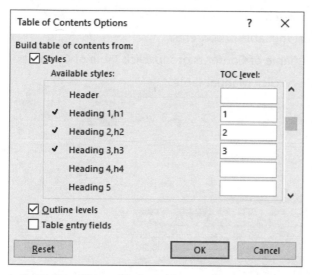

In the TOC Level list, specify the styles to include in the table of contents

In the Table Of Contents Options dialog box, check marks indicate the styles that Word uses to create the table of contents and the TOC level each style is associated with. You can include other styles in the table of contents by specifying a level in the TOC Level list. For example, to include sidebar headings as a fourth-level entry in a table of contents, enter 4 in the TOC Level list for the style Sidebar Heading.

By default, Word also uses outline levels to create a table of contents. You can assign an outline level to a style when you create or modify the style. For example, you might assign an outline level to a style you create for sidebar headings or captions so that you can view the content associated with these styles when you display a document in Outline view. To avoid including entries formatted with these styles when you insert a table of contents, clear the Outline Levels check box.

The Table Entry Fields check box in the Table Of Contents Options dialog box refers to headings or other elements of a document that have been manually marked to be included in the table of contents. When you manually mark content, Word inserts a TC field to mark the table of contents entry you selected. To include these manual entries in the table of contents, select the Table Entry Fields check box before you generate the table of contents.

Tip You can use the Add Text tool in the Table Of Contents group on the References tab to change the style applied to headings in a document. The Add Text tool displays the command Do Not Show In Table Of Contents and a list of the TOC levels that match the settings in the TOC Level list in the Table Of Contents Options dialog box (levels 1, 2, and 3, by default). You can, for example, apply the Heading 1 style to a paragraph formatted as Heading 2 by selecting the paragraph and then clicking Level 1 on the Add Text menu. If you select Do Not Show In Table Of Contents, Word will not show this heading when you generate the table of contents.

To build a table of contents from scratch

1. Click where you want to insert the table of contents.

2. On the **References** tab, in the **Table of Contents** group, click **Table of Contents**.

3. In the **Table of Contents** gallery, click **Manual Table**.

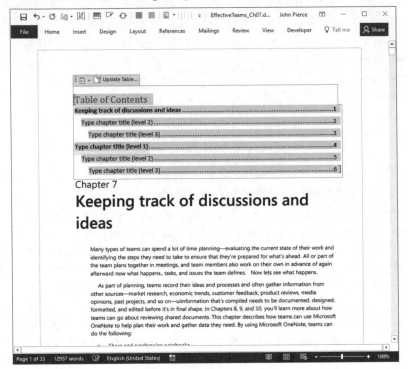

You can build a table of contents manually by typing the entries in placeholders Word provides

4. In the placeholders Word inserts, enter the headings for levels you want to include.

5. To insert additional placeholders, copy and paste a blank placeholder.

To create a custom table of contents

1. Click where you want to insert the table of contents.

2. On the **References** tab, in the **Table of Contents** group, click **Table of Contents**.

3. On the **Table of Contents** menu, click **Custom Table of Contents**.

4. In the **Table of Contents** dialog box, set options for showing and aligning page numbers, and choose the tab leader character and a table of contents format.

5. In the **Show Levels** box, enter or select the number of heading levels you want to include in the table of contents.

6. If you want to remove the hyperlinks from the table of contents headings, clear the **Use hyperlinks instead of page numbers** check box.

7. At the bottom of the **Table of Contents** dialog box, click **Options**.

8. In the **Table of Contents Options** dialog box, do any of the following:

   • To include other styles in the table of contents, specify the level in the **TOC Level** box to the right of the style name.

   • To exclude outline levels from the table of contents, clear the **Outline levels** check box.

   • To exclude styled elements from the table of contents, clear the **Styles** check box, and then use outline levels or table entry fields.

   • To include manually marked table entries, select the **Table entry fields** check box.

9. Click **OK** to insert the table of contents.

To open the Mark Table Of Contents Entry dialog box

➜ Press **Alt+Shift+O**.

To mark a table of contents entry manually

1. Select the heading or other text (such as a caption) you want to include in the table of contents.

2. Open the **Mark Table of Contents Entry** dialog box.

3. Verify that the **Table identifier** is set to C.

4. In the **Level** box, enter or select the level for the entry.

5. Click **Mark**.

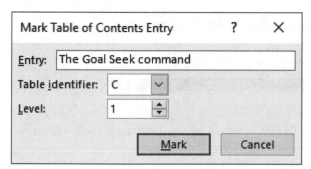

Manually marking content for inclusion in the table of contents

Caption and reference document elements

Descriptive captions are used to identify document elements such as illustrations, charts, tables, code listings, and equations. After captions are associated with a set of objects, you can generate reference tables (such as a table of figures) to include in a document. When you define a caption, you associate it with a specific element (a label) and can set options for how similar elements are numbered and how captions are positioned. Word applies its built-in Caption style to the captions you create.

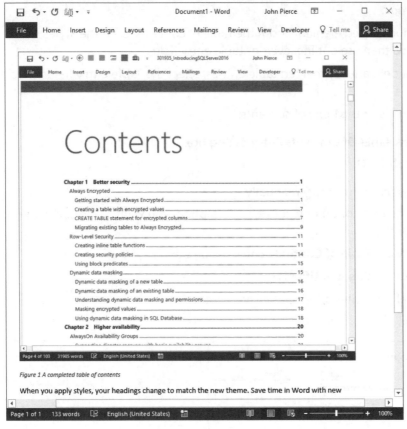

Add a caption to document elements such as figures and tables

The Insert Caption command in the Captions group opens the dialog box in which you enter a caption and define settings for how Word displays it.

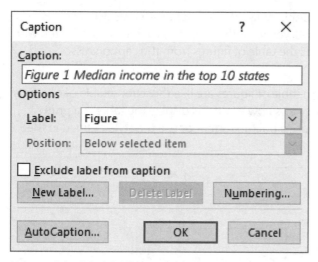

Use one of the default labels, or create your own

In the Caption dialog box, use the Label list to select the element you are adding a caption to (a figure, in this example). The default choices are Equation, Figure, and Table. You can define captions for other document elements (charts or maps, for example). You can delete custom labels when you no longer need them, but you cannot delete the default labels.

By clicking the Numbering button, you open the Caption Numbering dialog box. You can use the options in this dialog box to switch to a different numbering format (such as roman numerals) or to include a chapter number with a caption's label (for example, Table 3-3). Chapter headings must be defined by using one of the built-in heading styles. You can also select a character to separate the chapter number and the figure or table number. A hyphen is used by default; other choices include a period or a colon.

Tip If you often insert the same type of object in a document and you want these objects to have captions, click AutoCaption in the Caption dialog box. Select the type of object (such as Bitmap Image or Microsoft Excel Worksheet) that you want Word to provide a caption for when you insert an object of this type. You can select the label that's used with specific object types (or create a new label), where Word positions the caption by default, and specify how captions for this type of object are numbered.

If you need to modify a caption, you can edit the caption's text directly in the document or select the caption (including the label and number) and edit the caption in the Caption dialog box. With the Caption dialog box open, you can select a different label if needed, create a new label, or modify the numbering scheme for the captioned objects.

You can insert a table of figures to display a list of document elements with captions—tables, figures, equations, or elements you've added captions to that are associated with a label you defined. Word generates the table of figures from the captions associated with these objects.

The steps and options for creating a table of figures are like those for a table of contents. The Table Of Figures dialog box previews how Word will display the table in a printed document and online. You can choose a built-in format or use the style defined in the current template.

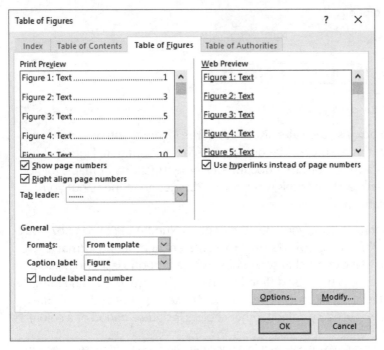

Use the Table Of Figures dialog box to create reference tables for figures, tables, and other captioned elements

In the Caption Label list, you select the label for the type of element you want to display in the table of figures. You can select None (in which case, numbered entries are preceded by *Caption*), Figure, Table, Equation, or a custom label you define by using the Caption dialog box.

By default, Word uses its built-in Caption style and the associated label to create the table of figures. Any element to which that style is applied and that is identified with that label is included. In the Table Of Figures Options dialog box, you can select a style to use as the basis for the entries in the table of figures or use table entries you have defined manually. As you can with table of content styles, you can modify the style Word uses to display the table of figures.

To create a caption for a document element

1. Select the object you want to create a caption for.

2. On the **References** tab, in the **Captions** group, click **Insert Caption**.

3. In the **Caption** dialog box, in the **Label** list, select the type of object.

4. In the **Caption** box, enter the caption after the label.

5. In the **Position** list, select an option for where you want to insert the caption.

> **IMPORTANT** The Position list is available only if you selected an object before opening the Caption dialog box.

6. Click **Numbering** to open the Caption Numbering dialog box, and then adjust number formatting for the caption.

7. Click **OK** in each of the open dialog boxes.

To create a custom label

1. On the **References** tab, in the **Captions** group, click **Insert Caption**.

2. In the **Caption** dialog box, click **New Label**.

3. Enter a name for the label, and then click **OK**.

To insert a table of figures

1. Click where you want to insert the table of figures.

2. On the **References** tab, in the **Captions** group, click **Insert Table of Figures**.

3. In the **Table of Figures** dialog box, set options for showing and aligning page numbers and choose the tab leader character and a table of figures format.

4. In the **Caption label** list, select the label you want to include with the captions.

5. If you want to remove hyperlinks from the table of figure entries, clear the **Use hyperlinks instead of page numbers** check box.

6. Click **OK** to insert the table of figures.

To set options for a table of figures

1. In the **Table of Figures** dialog box, click **Options**.

2. In the **Table of Figures Options** dialog box, do either of the following:

   - To base the table on a different style, select **Style**, and then choose a style from the list.

   - To include manually marked table entries, select **Table entry fields**.

3. Click **OK** in each of the open dialog boxes to insert the table.

Objective 3.2 practice tasks

The practice files for these tasks are located in the **MOSWordExpert2016 \Objective3** practice file folder. The folder also contains result files that you can use to check your work.

➤ Open the **WordExpert_3-2a** document and do the following:

❑ Insert a custom table of contents that shows entries for four heading levels (using TOC levels 1-4) and includes entries formatted with the Subtitle style (using TOC level 5).

➤ Save the **WordExpert_3-2a** document.

➤ Open the **WordExpert_3-2a_results** document. Compare the two documents to check your work. Then close the open documents.

➤ Open the **WordExpert_3-2b** document and do the following:

❑ In the first blank paragraph after each table, insert a caption using the built-in *Table* label. Accept the other default caption settings.

❑ In the blank paragraph after the *Tables* heading, insert a table of figures that references the table captions.

❑ In the blank paragraph after each picture, insert a caption that uses a custom Image label named *Word Screenshot*. Accept the other default caption settings.

❑ In the blank paragraph after the *Screenshots* heading, insert a table of figures that references the image captions.

➤ Save the **WordExpert_3-2b** document.

➤ Open the **WordExpert_3-2b_results** document. Compare the two documents to check your work. Then close the open documents.

Objective 3.3: Manage forms, fields, and mail-merge operations

This topic begins by describing how you can use fields and field properties to display information about a document or to automate information that is contained in document elements such as headers or footers. It also covers the steps you follow to set up and run a mail-merge operation, including how you manage a list of recipients.

Manage fields and their properties

As described earlier in this chapter, Word uses fields to manage elements such as indexes and tables of contents. Later in this section, you'll work with merge fields, which are used to specify information included in a mail merge.

In cases like these, Word inserts fields and sets field properties based on options you select in the user interface. You can also insert fields on your own to display information or to control how elements such as a table of contents appears.

The Field dialog box lists fields in categories such as Date And Time, Document Automation, Document Information, Links And References, and User Information. Fields that display document properties, such as author, keywords, and title, are listed in the Document Information category. You can display all fields or only the fields in a particular category.

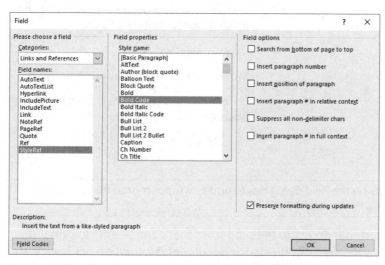

Set up a field by using the properties and options Word provides

3

When you select a field in the Field dialog box, a list of the field's properties is displayed. Field properties often control formatting—for example, whether the text displayed by a field is in all uppercase characters or which numbering or date format a field's data will use. Field properties also identify information such as which style to associate with the StyleRef field or the data source that's linked to the Database field.

Clicking the Field Codes button changes the display in the dialog box so that you see the field code. The field code includes the field's name (such as FileSize) and can also include properties and other switches that affect how the field's data is formatted and what the field displays. (The term *switch* refers generally to both field properties and options.) For example, the field code {FILESIZE * CardNumber \k * MERGEFORMAT} shows a document's file size as a cardinal number in kilobytes. The MERGEFORMAT switch indicates that the field's format remains the same when it is updated.

In a document, you can view the output of the field or the field code itself. When the information displayed in a field changes, you can update the field so that it's current. Word also provides keyboard shortcuts you can use to manage fields in a document, as shown in the following table.

Keyboard shortcut	Action
Ctrl+F9	Inserts a blank field
Alt+F9	Switches the view between field codes and field output for all fields in the document
Shift+F9	Switches the view between field codes and field output for selected fields
F9	Updates selected fields
F11 or Shift+F11	Moves to the next or previous field
Ctrl+F11	Locks a field and prevents it from being updated
Ctrl+Shift+F11	Unlocks a field

Tip Click the Help button in the Field dialog box to display a support page that provides a reference of field codes, properties, and options.

The Field dialog box provides access to the properties that control what information a field displays and how the field displays it. For document information fields such as Author, Keywords, and Title, you can select the Uppercase, Lowercase, First Capital, or Title Case property to specify how the text displayed by these fields appears. In the category Links And References, the properties for the StyleRef field is the list of styles in the document. You select the style that's associated with the text you want the field to display (a section heading in a document's footer, for example).

Selecting a property in the Field Properties area of the Field dialog box adds that property to the field code. You can modify the properties used with a field by displaying the field code and then opening the Field Options dialog box. Depending on the field you are working with, the Field Options dialog box provides a list of formatting options, general switches (which are also often related to the format in which a field displays data), and any field-specific switches (which are not included for every field). Keep in mind that some properties are not compatible with all fields or with other properties that field includes. You cannot, for example, apply a number format to text or add properties for two date formats to a single instance of a field.

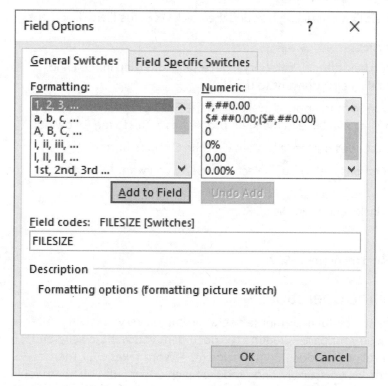

Use general and field-specific switches to modify a field's data and format

After you insert a field in a document, you can modify its properties by opening the Field dialog box from the menu displayed when you right-click the field.

To insert a field

1. On the **Insert** tab, in the **Text** group, click **Quick Parts**, and then click **Field**.

2. In the **Field** dialog box, select the field you want to insert. Use the **Categories** list to view a subset of the fields.

3. In the **Field properties** area, select properties to format the field's data or to identify the source (such as a style name, a file name, or an image file) for the field's data.

4. In the **Field options** area, select the options you want to use with the field.

5. To view the elements of the field code, click **Field Codes**.

6. Click **Options** to open the Field Options dialog box, and then select the properties and switches you want to apply.

7. Click **OK** in the **Field Options** dialog box, and then click **OK** in the **Field** dialog box.

To modify field properties

1. In the **Field** dialog box, filter by category if necessary, and then in the **Field names** list, select the field you want to use.

2. If the property you want to apply is available in the **Field properties** area, click it. If the property isn't available in the **Field properties** area, do the following:

   a. Click the **Field Codes** button, and then click the **Options** button.

   b. In the **Field Options** dialog box, select a property you want to apply to the field.

   c. Click **Add to Field**, and then click **OK**.

To update a field

→ Select the field, and then press **F9**.

Perform mail-merge operations

Viewing the results of a successful mail-merge operation can be very satisfying. After some preliminary work on your part—creating the document you want to send and identifying information about the document's recipients—Word takes over, merges the content and information you supply, and produces each document you need. You can incorporate additional options to control how Word produces the documents, and you aren't limited to producing paper mailings—you can send a personal email message to each recipient in a group by using the mail-merge features in Word.

Setting up and running a mail-merge operation entails six steps:

1. Open the document you want to use in the mail-merge operation, or start with a blank document and add text, illustrations, and other content. You can enter the content of the document later in the process, but you must have at least a blank document open to enable the commands you need on the Mailings tab.

2. Specify the type of mail-merge output you want to create—a letter, email message, envelope, sheet of labels, directory, or Word document.

> **Tip** A directory is like a catalog. It includes the same type of information about a group of items (for example, the name of each item, a description, and a price), but the information is distinct for each item.

3. Choose the source of your recipient list and select the specific recipients you want.

4. Insert merge fields in the document. During the mail-merge operation, Word replaces the merge fields with information from the recipient list.

5. Preview the results. You can find specific recipients or move from record to record in the list. Word can also check for errors in advance and compile those errors in a separate document.

6. Merge the document and recipient list. You can edit and save individual documents, print the documents all at once, or send the documents as email messages.

> **Tip** You can use the Step By Step Mail Merge Wizard to walk through the six mail-merge steps or perform them manually.

Manage recipient lists

Names, addresses, and other information you want to include about recipients in your mail-merge documents can come from a variety of sources. You can create an address list as a step in a mail-merge operation or use a list that's stored in a Microsoft Excel worksheet, a Microsoft Access database, your contacts list in Microsoft Outlook, or one of several other formats.

> **Tip** To be of best use in a mail merge, the information in an external data source should be organized as you need to use it for recipient information. For example, if you are compiling an address list in Excel, it's best to include a header row with column names that correspond to the fields Word uses for addresses in a mail-merge operation (such as *First*, *Last*, *Company*, *Mobile_Phone*, and so on).

3

The Type A New List option on the Select Recipients menu opens the New Address List dialog box, where you can compile a recipient list for the mail-merge operation. After you build the list, Word saves it in .mdb format. You can select this list for other mail-merge operations in the future.

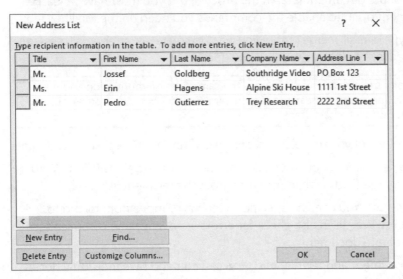

You can define your own columns for a recipient list

Scroll to the right in this dialog box to view the group of fields available by default. You can click the Customize Columns button to open a dialog box in which you can define additional fields, delete fields you don't need, rename fields, and change the order of the fields. By defining a custom field, you expand the type of information you can insert and display in a mail-merge operation. For example, you could create a field named Donation and enter the amount a recipient donated to your organization, or you could create a field named Auction Item and use it to describe what someone purchased at an auction. The amount of information you can store in a custom field is limited to 254 characters, including spaces.

In the New Address List dialog box, click a column heading to sort the list by that column, or click the arrow beside a column heading to open a menu to sort and filter the list in other ways. You can filter for a specific value, filter for blank values to fill in missing information, or click Advanced to open the Filter And Sort dialog box. On the Sort Records page in the Filter And Sort dialog box, you can specify as many as three fields to sort by. On the Filter Records page, you can set up a simple, single-field filter to find all records that equal (or do not equal) a specific value, or you can define multifield filters by using the OR and AND operators. Use the OR operator when you want to view records that match any of the conditions you define. Use the AND operator to select records that match both conditions you define.

The Comparison list on the Filter Records page includes the Less Than, Greater Than, Less Than Or Equal, Greater Than Or Equal, and other operators. You can use these operators to find records with specific numeric values in a custom field you create. For example, for a mail-merge operation related to a fundraising campaign, you could create and populate a custom field named Pledge or Donation and then filter on the values for that field (pledges above $1,000, for example) to send a document only to those recipients. For text fields such as names and locations (city or country/ region, for example) or a field such as Zip Code, you can use the Contains or Does Not Contain operators to find recipients who live in a specific area or whose last name is Lambert.

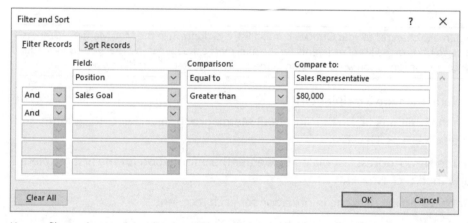

You can filter and sort recipient lists by multiple criteria

If you select an Excel workbook or an Access database as the source of a recipient list, Word opens the Select Table dialog box. This dialog box lists each worksheet and named range in an Excel workbook or the tables and queries defined in an Access database. In this dialog box, you can select the worksheet, range, or database object you want to use.

A Word document that contains nothing but a table is also a valid source of data for a recipient list. You can set up the table with the column headings you want to use for fields in the mail merge.

If the information you want to use for the recipient list is stored in a server database (for example, a Microsoft SQL Server database), you can use the Data Connection wizard to create a connection. As you step through the wizard, you need to provide information such as the server name and the user name and password required to gain access to the server. Choosing the Other/Advanced option in the wizard opens the Data Link Properties dialog box. In this dialog box, you select a data source provider and specify the information and other initialization properties required to make a connection. You might need to obtain some of this information from a network or server administrator.

If you maintain and manage a detailed contacts list in Outlook—including information such as company names, phone numbers, mailing addresses, and other details—you can make productive use of your contacts folder as the data source for a mail-merge operation. All the contacts in the folder you choose are selected for the operation by default.

Tip If you make changes to your Outlook contact list, click Refresh in the Mail Merge Recipients dialog box to update the list of recipients for the mail merge. Keep in mind that you cannot edit Outlook contact information while working in the Mail Merge Recipients dialog box.

To create and manage a recipient list

1. On the **Mailings** tab, in the **Start Mail Merge** group, click **Select Recipients**, and then click **Type New List**.

2. In the **New Address List** dialog box, enter the information for the first recipient and then click **New Entry**.

3. Repeat step 2 to add the information for each recipient.

4. In the **New Address List** dialog box, click **OK**.

5. In the **Save Address List** dialog box, open the folder you want to save the recipient list in, and then click **Save**.

To modify a recipient list

1. In the **New Address List** dialog box, click **Customize Columns**.

2. Do any of the following:

   - To add a custom field, click **Add**, enter the name of the field in the **Add Field** dialog box, and then click **OK**.

   - To change the order of the fields, select the field you want to move and then click **Move Up** or **Move Down**.

- To locate a specific recipient in the list, click **Find**. In the **Find Entry** dialog box, enter the text string you want Word to find. This might be a first name, a last name, a city name, or a value related to a different field. To search for this text in a specific field, click **This Field** and then choose the field you want to search. Click **Find Next**. Click **Cancel** when you locate the field you are looking for.

- To delete an entry, select the row, and then click **Delete Entry**.

To select an external data source

1. On the **Mailings** tab, in the **Start Mail Merge** group, click **Select Recipients**, and then click **Use Existing List**.

2. In the **Select Data Source** dialog box, open the folder that contains the data source file you want to use.

> **IMPORTANT** If the dialog box doesn't display the data source file, select the format or All Files (*.*) in the Files Of Type list.

3. Select the data source file, and then click **Open**.

4. If the **Select Table** dialog box opens, choose the worksheet, cell range, or database object that contains the recipient information you want, and then click **OK**.

To use an Outlook contact folder as a recipient list

1. On the **Mailings** tab, in the **Start Mail Merge** group, click **Select Recipients**, and then click **Choose From Outlook Contacts**.

2. If prompted, choose the Outlook profile that is associated with the contacts folder you want to use.

3. In the **Select Contacts** dialog box, select the contacts folder you want to use, and then click **OK**.

4. In the **Mail Merge Recipients** dialog box, clear the check box to the left of any contact you don't want to include in the mail merge.

5. If you want to refresh the list so that it shows recent changes made in Outlook, select **Contacts** in the **Data Source** pane, and then click **Refresh**.

Modify recipient lists

After you choose a recipient list, you can edit or filter it to include only specific recipients, and sort it to set the order of the merged documents or labels. For example, you might want to sort by city or by company for a mailing you are preparing for specific clients or locales.

3

You can locate specific contacts or duplicate contacts within the recipient list. For certain types of data sources (such as Excel workbooks and Access databases, but not for Outlook contact lists), you can edit detailed information about recipients when the recipient list is displayed.

To edit a recipient list

1. On the **Mailings** tab, in the **Start Mail Merge** group, click **Edit Recipient List**.

2. In the **Mail Merge Recipients** dialog box, select the recipient list in the **Data Source** area, and then click **Edit**.

3. In the **Edit Data Source** dialog box, update the values for fields, or click **New Entry** to add a recipient record.

4. In the **Edit Data Source** dialog box, click **OK**. In the message box Word displays, click **Yes** to update the recipient list and save the changes to the original data source.

To refine a recipient list

1. On the **Mailings** tab, in the **Start Mail Merge** group, click **Edit Recipient List**.

2. In the **Mail Merge Recipients** dialog box, do any of the following:

   - Use the arrows beside column headings to sort the list by that field (in ascending or descending order) or to filter the list by values in that field or for blank or nonblank fields.

   - For more advanced sorts, in the **Refine Recipient List** area, click **Sort** to open the Filter And Sort dialog box. On the **Sort Records** tab, you can sort by up to three fields.

   - To define an advanced filter, in the **Refine Recipient List** area, click **Filter**. On the **Filter Records** page of the **Filter and Sort** dialog box, select the field you want to filter by. Select a comparison operator, and then enter the text you want to use for the filter. In the far-left column, you can also select the AND or OR operator and then add another field to the filter. Repeat this step to define other conditions for the filter.

   - To check for duplicate recipients, click **Find Duplicates**. In the **Find Duplicates** dialog box, clear the check box beside the duplicate entries you don't want to include.

   - To locate a specific recipient, click **Find Recipient**. In the **Find Entry** dialog box, enter the text you want Word to search for. To search in a specific field, select **This Field**, and then select the field you want to use.

3. In the **Mail Merge Recipients** dialog box, click **OK**.

Insert merge fields

Merge fields correspond to the columns of information in a recipient list. To add the information stored in a recipient list to a document, you insert merge fields where you want the information to appear in the document. You can place the information at the start of the document to define an address block or a greeting, and within the body of the document, where you might include a company name or other information.

Word provides composite merge fields for an address block and a greeting line. The Address Block command in the Write & Insert Fields group inserts standard information such as title, first and last names, mailing address, city, state, country/region, and postal code. In the Insert Address Block dialog box, you can tailor the address block so that it fits the needs of the mail-merge operation you have underway.

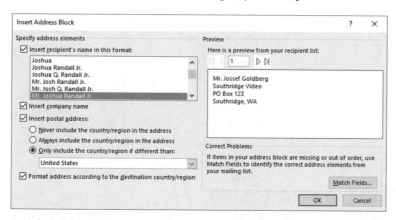

By default, address blocks include all possible elements

The ways you can modify the standard address block include the following:

- Choose a format for recipient names (first name only, first and last names, first and last names with title, and others).

- Clear the Insert Company Name check box if you don't want to include that information. (The check box is selected by default.)

- Clear the Insert Postal Address check box. For example, you might want only names to appear in the document and use address information for labels or envelopes. You can also specify under what conditions you want the country /region name to appear in the address block.

The Greeting Line command presents similar kinds of options. You can alter the salutation from Dear to To, for example, and specify how recipient names appear. Use the Greeting Line For Invalid Recipient Names list to choose a greeting that Word applies when information in the recipient list doesn't match the format you choose for a name.

You add individual merge fields, including any custom fields you define when building a recipient list, to a document by choosing the fields from the Insert Merge Field list or by using the options in the Insert Merge Field dialog box. In the dialog box, the Address Fields option displays an extended list of fields. The Database Fields option displays the fields defined in the associated recipient list.

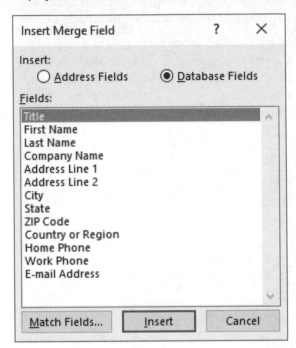

Insert merge fields from this dialog box to include recipient information in the mail merge

You can insert merge fields at any place in the document that makes sense. For example, in the final paragraph of a letter, you might repeat the recipient's first name for emphasis—"In closing, I want to thank you again, <<First_Name>>, for your support of our campaign."

If the fields in an Excel worksheet or other data source you are using for recipient information don't correspond precisely with the fields in Word, use the Match Fields command in the Write & Insert Fields group to open a dialog box in which you can set up the field relationships you need. (You can also open this dialog box by clicking the Match Fields button in the Insert Address Block or Insert Greeting Line dialog box.) In the Match Fields dialog box, if a field in your data source doesn't match a field in Word, Word displays Not Matched. Keep in mind that you cannot include any unmatched fields in the mail-merge document. You can save the configuration of matching fields if you expect to use this data source for other mail-merge operations on the computer you are using.

Tip You don't need to complete a mail-merge operation in one sitting. You can save a document you are preparing for a mail-merge operation, and Word maintains the association with the data source for recipients and any merge fields you have inserted. When you open the document to begin work again, click Yes in the message box that Word displays to confirm that you want to open the document and run an SQL command.

The Preview Results command inserts recipient records into the merge fields so that you can see how each document will appear. You can use the Find Recipient command to locate a specific recipient, or use the preview arrows to move from record to record in the recipient list.

Word can check for errors before you print documents or run your mail merge via email. The dialog box that Word displays provides three options: simulating the merge and reporting errors in a new document, running the merge and pausing if Word encounters an error, and completing the merge and reporting errors in a separate document. The types of errors Word checks for include missing information in the recipient list.

To insert an address block merge field

1. In the document, click where you want to insert the address block.
2. On the **Mailings** tab, in the **Write & Insert Fields** group, click **Address Block**.
3. In the **Insert Address Block** dialog box, do any of the following:
   - In the **Insert recipient's name in this format** pane, click the format you want to use for recipient names.
   - To exclude names from the address block, clear the **Insert recipient's name in this format** check box.
   - To exclude the company name or postal address, clear the corresponding check box.
   - If you include the postal address, select an option for when to include the country/region name in the address block.
   - If you want to use the same format for all addresses, clear the **Format address according to the destination country/region** check box.
4. In the **Preview** area, review the effect of your choices on the content and structure of the addresses.

To insert a greeting line merge field

1. In the document, click where you want to insert the greeting line.
2. On the **Mailings** tab, in the **Write & Insert Fields** group, click **Greeting Line**.

3

3. In the **Insert Greeting Line** dialog box, do either of the following:

   • Specify a format for the elements of the greeting line, including the saluta-tion and name format.

   • Choose a format for invalid recipient names.

4. In the **Preview** area, review the effect of your choices on the content and struc-ture of the greeting line.

To insert a merge field

1. In the document, click where you want to insert the merge field.

2. On the **Mailings** tab, in the **Write & Insert Fields** group, do either of the following:

   • Click the **Insert Merge Field** arrow, and then click the field you want to insert.

   • Click the **Insert Merge Field** button. In the **Insert Merge Field** dialog box, click the field you want to insert, and then click **Insert**.

To match merge fields with recipient list fields

1. On the **Mailings** tab, in the **Write & Insert Fields** group, click **Match Fields**.

2. In the **Match Fields** dialog box, in the list on the right, select a field from your recipient list to match the field names Word provides in the list on the left.

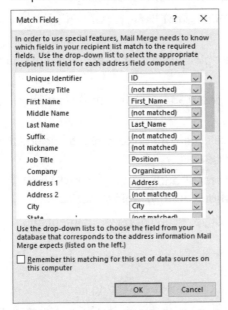

Use this dialog box to match fields in your recipient list with merge fields in Word

3. Click **OK**.

To preview mail-merge results

1. On the **Mailings** tab, in the **Preview Results** group, click **Preview Results**.

2. In the **Preview Results** group, do any of the following:

   - Click the arrows to show the first, next, previous, or last mail-merge record.

   - Click **Find Recipient**. In the **Find Record** dialog box, enter the text you want to search for, and then click **Find Next**.

   - Click **Check For Errors**, and then select the option you want to use.

Add mail-merge rules

Mail-merge rules enable you to define conditional elements that can add flexibility and help customize records produced in a mail-merge operation. The rules are listed on the Rules menu in the Write & Insert Fields group.

One helpful rule is the If Then Else rule. With this rule, you can specify an IF condition (for example, "If the State field is equal to California") and then enter the text you want Word to insert when the condition you define is true and alternative text that Word inserts when the IF condition is false.

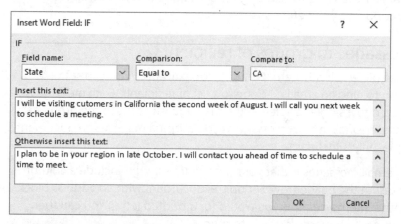

You can set up mail-merge rules to customize content based on conditions you define

Two other rules you might make use of are Ask and Fill In. These rules can prompt you as each mail-merge document is produced so that you can change information on the fly. You set up an Ask rule to prompt you or another user to enter text at a specific location. The Ask rule uses a bookmark you create to mark the location in the document. For example, you might create a bookmark named Discount where you want to specify the discount that a customer is going to receive. You can then enter a prompt that lets you or another user know what text to enter. You can also define the text you want to display by default. In the Insert Word Field: Ask dialog box, you can select the Ask Once check box if you want to be prompted only at the start of the final mail merge. Keep the check box cleared if you want the prompt to appear for each record. When you start merging documents, you'll be prompted to accept the default text or insert an alternative for the document being produced. The Fill-In rule works similarly.

To define an If Then Else mail-merge rule

1. On the **Mailings** tab, in the **Write & Insert Fields** group, click **Rules**, and then click **If...Then...Else...**

2. In the **Insert Word Field: If** dialog box, do the following and then click **OK**:

    a. In the **Field name** list, select the field you want to use in an IF condition.

    b. In the **Comparison** list, select a comparison operator.

    c. In the **Compare to** box, enter the text or other value you want to compare the field with.

    d. In the **Insert this text** box, enter the text that you want Word to insert when the IF condition is true.

    e. In the **Otherwise insert this text** box, enter the text that should appear when the condition you define is false.

Send email messages to groups of recipients

If you have a compatible email program (Outlook, for example), you can set up a mail-merge operation to send an email message to a list of recipients. Each message is a single item addressed to a single recipient—the message isn't sent to the group as a whole—and you can personalize each message as you might a mail-merge document by using, for example, only a first name.

One key in sending email messages is that your data source should include a column labeled E-Mail Address in the header row. Set up the document with an address block, greeting line, and other merge fields as you would for a printed letter. You can then preview the results of each message you plan to send.

To send an email message as a mail-merge document

1. Create the document you want to send as an email message.

2. Select or build the recipient list, insert merge fields, and define merge rules as necessary.

3. On the **Mailings** tab, in the **Finish** group, click **Finish & Merge**, and then click **Send Email Messages**.

4. In the **Merge to E-mail** dialog box, do the following and then click **OK**:

   a. In the **To** list, select the field that contains the recipients' email addresses.

   b. In the **Subject line** box, enter the text that you want to appear in the message subject field.

   c. In the **Message format** list, click **Attachment**, **Plain text**, or **HTML**.

   d. In the **Send records** area, select the recipient records you want to send the message to.

Configure label or envelope settings for mail-merge operations

The Mailings tab provides a couple of ways to configure settings for labels and envelopes and then print on them. You can use the Envelopes or Labels option on the Start Mail Merge menu to merge information from your recipient list to produce the envelope or label setup you need. You can use the Envelopes and Labels commands in the Create group (at the far left of the Mailings tab) to prepare and print these items without setting up a full mail-merge operation.

When you are preparing to print on labels or envelopes as part of a mail-merge operation, start with a blank document. If you have a document open when you select either option from the Start Mail Merge menu, Word displays a warning telling you that it must delete the contents of the open document and discard any changes before it can continue.

Depending on the options you select for envelopes or labels (envelope size, for example, or label vendor and product number), Word displays a document with an area in which you insert merge fields. You can enter or select a recipient list, and then add the merge fields you want to include on the envelopes or labels. You can use the Address Block command, for example, or add individual merge fields. You can also add merge rules. For example, you might add the Merge Record # rule as a way to determine how many labels or envelopes you print.

With merge fields in place, you can preview the results and then use the Finish & Merge menu to print on the labels or envelopes.

3

To configure and print on envelopes

1. Start with a blank document.

2. On the **Start Mail Merge** menu, click **Envelopes**.

3. In the **Envelope Options** dialog box, do the following and then click **OK**:

   a. Select the envelope size.

   b. Change the font formatting for the addresses as needed.

   c. On the **Printing Options** tab, check that the settings are correct for the printer you are using.

4. Click **Select Recipients**, and then choose an option for the recipient list you want to use.

5. Add merge fields to the envelope to create an address block.

6. Preview the results, and check for any errors.

7. Click **Finish & Merge**, and then click **Print Documents**.

To configure and print on labels

1. Start with a blank document.

2. On the **Start Mail Merge** menu, click **Labels**.

3. In the **Label Options** dialog box, do the following and then click **OK**:

   a. Select the type of printer you are using.

   b. In the **Label Information** area, select the label vendor and then the product number for the label you are using.

4. Click **Select Recipients**, and then choose an option for the recipient list you want to use.

5. Add merge fields to the document to create an address block.

6. Preview the results, and check for any errors.

7. Click **Finish & Merge**, and then click **Print Documents**.

Objective 3.3 practice tasks

The practice files for these tasks are located in the **MOSWordExpert2016 \Objective3** practice file folder. The folder also contains result files that you can use to check your work.

➤ Open the **WordExpert_3-3a** document and do the following:

- ❑ At the beginning of the file, insert the <u>Author</u>, <u>Keywords</u>, and <u>NumChars</u> fields.

- ❑ Apply a field property so that the keywords appear in uppercase.

➤ Save the **WordExpert_3-3a** document.

➤ Open the **WordExpert_3-3a_results** document. Compare the two documents to check your work. Then close the open documents.

➤ Open the **WordExpert_3-3b** document and do the following:

- ❑ Choose the option to use an existing list as the recipient list. Select the **WordExpert_3-3c** workbook.

- ❑ Use the Match Fields command to match the *Organization* field to the *Company* field. Set the *Courtesy Title* field to *Unmatched*.

- ❑ Edit the recipient list by changing the entry for Jan Kotas to Jossef Goldberg.

- ❑ Insert a greeting block, and insert the *First_Name* field after the opening salutation.

- ❑ Insert the *Sales_Goal* field in the highlighted area of the document. Delete the highlighted text.

- ❑ Create an If Then Else merge rule for the *Sales Goal* field that inserts the text <u>Way to go!</u> for the records in which the sales goal is greater than $80,000. For other records, use the text <u>Keep trying</u>.

- ❑ Preview the records.

➤ Save the **WordExpert_3-3b** document. Open the **WordExpert_3-3b_ results** document. Compare the two documents to check your work. Then close the open documents.

Objective group 4

Create custom Word elements

The skills tested in this section of the Microsoft Office Specialist Expert exam for Microsoft Word 2016 relate to creating custom Word elements, including building blocks, macros, themes, and style sets. Specifically, the following objectives are associated with this set of skills:

4.1 Create and modify building blocks, macros, and controls

4.2 Create custom style sets and templates

4.3 Prepare a document for internationalization and accessibility

Documents often have specific requirements. For example, a series of documents might require a common appearance or regularly include a content element such as a cover page or a disclaimer. You can create and save elements such as custom themes and building blocks to more efficiently work with these requirements. You also need to consider the scope of a document's audience and how to make document elements accessible and easier to understand by readers who don't speak your native language. And if you often perform a specific set of steps when you create or modify a document, you can record a macro to perform those steps for you.

This chapter guides you in studying ways to create and modify building blocks, macros, and controls; create custom style sets and templates; and prepare documents for internationalization and accessibility.

4

To complete the practice tasks in this chapter, you need the practice files contained in the **MOSWordExpert2016\Objective4** practice file folder. For more information, see "Download the practice files" in this book's introduction.

Objective 4.1: Create and modify building blocks, macros, and controls

Building blocks, macros, and controls—in different ways and to different degrees—enable you to automate the insertion of document elements and more easily accomplish repetitive tasks. These three element types are described more fully in the following list:

- Word provides building blocks for document elements such as headers and footers, cover pages, and tables. Galleries that you display by selecting commands on the ribbon are filled with these and other types of building blocks. You can create your own building blocks, save them in a gallery, and then use them again in related documents. For example, Quick Parts are a type of building block you can use to insert text or other document elements you use repeatedly. You can insert a logo or the text of a standard disclaimer in a document and then save this element to the Quick Part gallery, where it appears when you need to insert the Quick Part in a document. You can also edit the properties of building blocks.

- You can use macros to automate tasks such as applying or replacing styles and formatting, applying a set of page-layout options, entering or deleting text, or navigating a document.

- In specific types of documents, especially forms, you can add and define content controls to manage input and data collection. Content controls such as list boxes or combo boxes are similar to the types of controls that appear regularly in dialog boxes.

This section describes how to create a Quick Part, edit and manage building blocks, record and edit a simple macro, and insert and configure content controls.

Create Quick Parts

Quick Parts can cover a range of elements that you use in multiple documents or repeatedly within the same document. By creating a Quick Part, you make a document element available directly from a gallery on the Insert tab. A Quick Part might contain a standard caption you use with figures or tables, a heading that is followed by place-holder text, a brief legal disclaimer, or a logo you insert at the top of correspondence or a report.

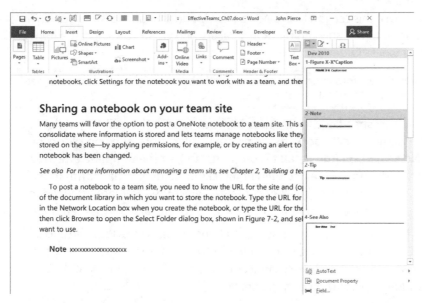

Create and save a Quick Part to add common elements to a document by using a gallery

When you create a Quick Part (or another type of building block), you use the options in the Create New Building Block dialog box to name the Quick Part and specify other properties. By default, Word saves Quick Parts and other building blocks in a template file named *Building Blocks.dotx*. By saving a custom building block to that file (or to the standard Normal template—Normal.dotm), you make the building block available to all new documents. You can also save a building block in the template file attached to a document. The building block is then available to any document you create based on that template.

When you create a new building block, you can specify the following properties:

- **Name** The name of the building block. You can insert a Quick Part by typing the first several characters in its name and then pressing Enter when prompted by Word.

- **Gallery** The gallery in which you want the building block to appear. Use the built-in galleries (such as Quick Part or Cover Page) or one of the galleries Word provides named Custom. You cannot enter your own gallery name.

- **Category** You can assign a building block to a category within a gallery. Items in a gallery are grouped by their category. Select Create New Category in this list to define a custom category.

4

- **Description** Use this section to provide a description that appears in a ScreenTip when you point to the building block in a gallery and when you select the item in the Building Blocks Organizer.

  > **See Also** For more information about working with the Building Blocks Organizer, see "Manage building blocks" later in this topic.

- **Save in** This box specifies the template in which to save the building block. You can select Building Blocks.dotx (the template used to store building blocks by default), Normal.dotm (the default Word template), or the template attached to the current document. Select Building Blocks.dotx (or Normal.dotm) to make the building block available to all documents. Select the template attached to the current document to create a building block specifically for that template.

- **Options** These options specify how the building block is inserted. The choices are Insert Content Only, Insert Content In Its Own Paragraph, and Insert Content In Its Own Page. The first of these choices places the building block at the cursor without adding a paragraph or page break.

To create a Quick Part

1. Select the content you want to include in the Quick Part.

2. On the **Insert** tab, in the **Text group**, click **Quick Parts**, and then click **Save Selection to Quick Part Gallery**.

3. In the **Create New Building Block** dialog box, enter a name and a description for the Quick Part.

4. Select the gallery and category in which you want the Quick Part to appear.

5. In the **Save in** list, do either of the following:

   - To make the Quick Part available to all documents, click **Building Blocks.dotx**.

   - To include the Quick Part only in the template attached to the document, click that template.

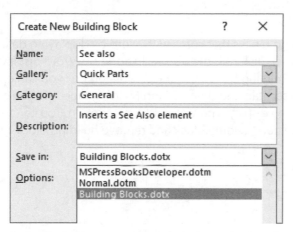

Saving the Quick Part to Building Blocks.dotx makes it available to all new documents

6. In the **Options** list, select the option you want to use to insert the Quick Part: **Insert content only**, **Insert content in its own paragraph**, or **Insert content in its own page**.

7. Click **OK** to apply the settings.

To insert a Quick Part in a document

→ Enter the name of the Quick Part, and then press **F3**.

Or

1. On the **Insert** tab, in the **Text** group, click **Quick Parts**.

2. In the **Quick Parts** gallery, do one of the following:

   • Click a Quick Part to insert it by using the default insertion option.

   • Right-click a Quick Part, and then click one of the following insertion options:

     ○ **Insert at Current Document Position**

     ○ **Insert at Page Header**

     ○ **Insert at Page Footer**

     ○ **Insert at Beginning of Section**

     ○ **Insert at End of Section**

     ○ **Insert at Beginning of Document**

     ○ **Insert at End of Document**

Manage building blocks

You can view the range of building blocks that come with Word by displaying galleries (such as for cover pages or watermarks) from the ribbon. In addition, Word displays the list of building blocks in the Building Blocks Organizer, a dialog box you can open by clicking Quick Parts on the Insert tab and then clicking Building Blocks Organizer. Select a building block in the list to display a preview and a description. You can then modify the properties of the selected building block and remove building blocks you no longer need.

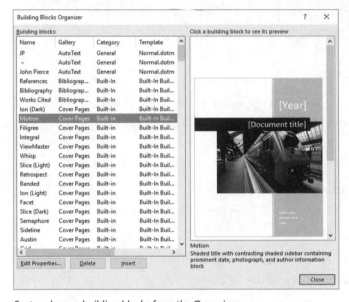

Sort and move building blocks from the Organizer

Each building block is defined by a set of properties that you can use to keep building blocks organized and to specify how Word inserts the building block. In the Modify Building Block dialog box, you can change the gallery a building block is assigned to, update its category, modify its description, and change other properties.

See Also For a detailed description of building block properties, see "Create Quick Parts" earlier in this topic.

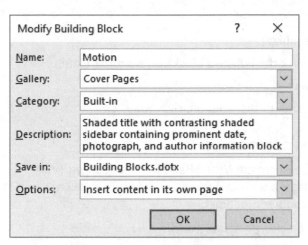

Modify a building block to save it in a different location or in a different category

To open the Building Blocks Organizer

→ On the **Insert** tab, in the **Text** group, click **Quick Parts**, and then click **Building Blocks Organizer**.

→ In the **Quick Parts** gallery, right-click a building block, and then click **Organize and Delete**.

To open the Modify Building Block dialog box for a building block

→ In the **Quick Parts** gallery, right-click the building block you want to modify, and then click **Edit Properties**.

→ Open the **Building Blocks Organizer**. In the **Building blocks** pane, click the building block you want to modify. Then click **Edit Properties**.

To edit building block properties

1. Open the **Modify Building Block** dialog box for the building block that you want to modify.

2. Update the **Name**, **Gallery**, **Category**, **Description**, **Save In**, or **Options** properties, and then click **OK**.

3. When Word prompts you to redefine the building block entry, click **Yes**.

4

To delete a building block

1. Open the **Building Blocks Organizer**.
2. In the **Building blocks** pane, click the building block you want to delete.
3. Below the **Building blocks** pane, click **Delete**.
4. When Word prompts you to confirm the deletion, click **Yes**.

Create and modify simple macros

A macro is a procedure that uses the Microsoft Visual Basic for Applications (VBA) programming language. A procedure is a series of instructions that are saved as a unit, which can then be performed as a single instruction.

```
MSPressBooks_Begin_to_Code - modCodeStyles (Code)
(General)                                          ApplyCodeStyles
        If Selection.End = ActiveDocument.Content.End Then
            EndOfDoc = True
        Else
            EndOfDoc = False
        End If
End Function

Private Sub Convert(sCodeStyle As String)
Selection.HomeKey Unit:=wdStory
    Do
        ClearFindReplace
        Selection.Find.Style = sCodeStyle
        Selection.Find.Execute

        If Selection.Find.Found And Not EndOfDoc Then
            If Selection.End - Selection.Start > 1 Then
                With Selection.range.Find
                    .ClearFormatting
                    .Font.Color = wdColorBlue
                    .Replacement.Style = ActiveDocument.Styles("CodeBlue")
                    .Execute Replace:=wdReplaceAll
                End With
                With Selection.range.Find
                    .ClearFormatting
                    .Font.Color = wdColorGreen
                    .Replacement.Style = ActiveDocument.Styles("CodeGreen")
                    .Execute Replace:=wdReplaceAll
                End With
                With Selection.range.Find
```

This macro substitutes character styles for local font colors

In Word, you can record a series of commands (including settings you select in a dialog box) or keystrokes as a macro. When you create a macro, you perform the series of actions that completes a task or a portion of a task that you want to automate, and Word records the tasks. You can then run the macro and have Word perform the tasks for you.

IMPORTANT While you record a macro, you can use the mouse to invoke commands but not to select objects, because selecting an object with the mouse isn't a step that Word can re-create.

The first step in recording a macro is to specify settings for the macro, including a name and a location. You can save a macro in Normal.dotm, which makes the macro available in all documents, or in the template file that is attached to the current document. You can assign a macro to a keyboard shortcut or to a button that you can place on the Quick Access Toolbar or on the ribbon.

Before you record a macro, it can be helpful to rehearse the steps you want to record. As an example, you might record a macro that applies a set of page-layout options, such as inserting a section break and setting the margins, page orientation, and header for the section. You could run a macro such as this in documents whose content requires pages that use the Landscape orientation (to display a wide table, for example) in addition to pages that retain the Portrait orientation. As preparation for recording the macro, walk through the options that you want to apply and the sequence in which you want to apply them.

See Also For more information about page layout options, see "Set advanced page layout options" in "Objective 2.1: Perform advanced editing and formatting."

You can take your time performing the actions while recording the macro because Word doesn't record the timing. You can pause recording when you need to determine which command or option to select next or to modify a setting that you have already selected. When you pause recording, you can effectively edit the macro (so that it applies the correct setting) without having to work directly with the VBA code that is generated by Word.

You can edit a macro that you have recorded by opening the Visual Basic for Applications editor and code window. In the code window, you might change the font color the macro applies, for example, or change the text that is used in a find-and-replace operation you performed when you recorded the macro.

To open the Record Macro dialog box

→ On the **View** tab, in the **Macros** group, click **Record Macro**.

→ On the **Developer** tab, in the **Code** group, click **Record Macro**.

→ On the status bar, click the **Macro Recording** button.

Tip The Developer tab is hidden by default. You display the Developer tab from the Customize Ribbon page of the Word Options dialog box. For information about displaying hidden tabs, see "Change default program settings" in "Objective 1.1: Manage documents and templates."

4

To record a macro

1. Open the **Record Macro** dialog box.

2. In the **Macro name** box, enter a descriptive name for the macro.

> **Tip** Macro names cannot contain spaces. They can contain numbers, and words can be separated by an underscore character (_).

3. In the **Store macro in** list, select the template or document in which you want to save the macro.

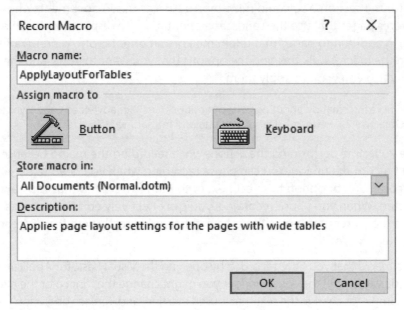

Give macros names that describe their purposes

4. If you want to save a description of the macro, enter it in the **Description** box.

5. Click **OK**, and then perform the steps you want to record in the macro.

6. On the **View** tab, in the **Macros** group, click **Stop Recording**.

To pause and resume recording

1. On the **View** tab, in the **Macros** group, click **Pause Recording**.

2. Correct the previous setting or determine the next action to take.

3. On the **View** tab, in the **Macros** group, click **Resume Recording**.

To open the Macros dialog box

→ On the **View** tab, in the **Macros** group, click **View Macros**.

→ On the **Developer** tab, in the **Code** group, click **Macros**.

To edit a macro

1. Open the **Macros** dialog box.

2. In list of macros, select the macro you want to change, and then click **Edit** to open the Visual Basic for Applications code window.

3. In the code window, edit the code statement you want to change.

4. Close the code window, and then close the Visual Basic for Applications window.

Insert and configure content controls

To help build documents that capture user input (forms, for example), you can insert and configure a variety of content controls, including a text box, list box, or check box. You use content controls to manage input by specifying items for a list, for example, or by providing a defined set of options related to check boxes.

Content controls display a simple text statement that tells users what to do with the control. For example, text controls display *Click or tap here to enter text*, and the date-picker control prompts users to *Click or tap to enter a date*. You can customize this text so that it provides precise instructions and helps users work with a control more efficiently.

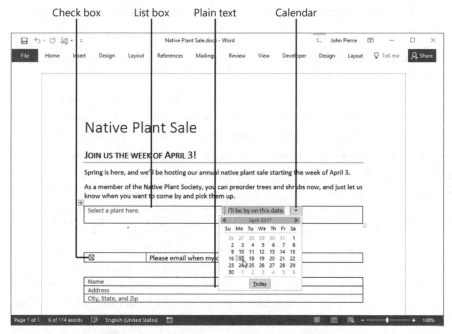

A document that contains multiple content controls

The content controls you can add to a document are displayed in the Controls group on the Developer tab. The following content controls are available:

- **Rich text** Use this control for text fields in which you need to format text as bold or italic, for example, or if you need to include multiple paragraphs and add other content such as images and tables.

- **Plain text** Use the plain-text control for simple text fields such as names, addresses, or job titles. The text added to a plain-text control can be formatted only in limited ways, and the control can include only a single paragraph by default.

- **Picture** Use this control to embed an image file in a document. You can use a picture control to display a logo, for example, or pictures of project personnel.

- **Building block gallery** Use a building block gallery control when you want users of the document to have access to a specific block of text saved as a Quick Part or to AutoText entries, equations, or tables from those respective building block galleries. You can also select a custom gallery.

  In a request for proposal document, for example, you might include a building block control from which users choose text entries from the Quick Parts gallery to indicate the length of time for which the proposal is valid. You choose which gallery the content control is associated with in the properties dialog box for the control.

  See Also For more information about building blocks, see "Create Quick Parts" and "Manage building blocks" earlier in this topic. For information about control properties, read further in this section.

- **Check box** Use the check box control to provide a set of options—product sizes, for example, or options that indicate which events a user plans to attend.

- **Combo box** In a combo box, users can select from a list of defined choices or enter their own information. If you lock a combo box control, users cannot add their own items to the list.

  See Also For more information about locking controls, read further in this section.

- **Drop-down list** In this control, users can select only from a list of defined options. You might use a drop-down list to display department names, meeting rooms, or product names (a list of specific items). A combo box is better suited for displaying a list of tasks, so that users can select a task if it appears on the list or define one if it doesn't.

- **Date picker** This control inserts a calendar control that lets users select or enter a date.
- **Repeating section** A repeating section content control can guide readers in entering the same information in multiple sections. You can also nest other content controls (such as a text box) within a repeating section control. You could use this content control in a table, for example, to alert users of a document about what information should be inserted in each column in each row.

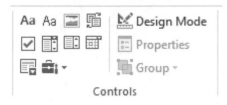

Document content controls

Tip Pointing to a content control in the Controls group on the Developer tab displays a ScreenTip that identifies the control.

Tip To group content controls, select the controls, and then click Group in the Controls group on the Developer tab. For example, you can group a set of check boxes so that they cannot be edited or deleted individually.

Each content control has a set of properties. The most basic properties are Title and Tag. Word displays a control's title to identify it. The Tag property helps you locate a control and can be used if you link a control to a data source. Tags also enclose controls when you work in design mode.

Properties also affect how the contents of a control are formatted, whether the control can be deleted, and whether its content can be edited. Other properties depend on the type of control you are working with. For example, for a plain text control, you can set an option to allow multiple paragraphs.

4

Properties for the date-picker control include the date format, the locale, and the calendar type.

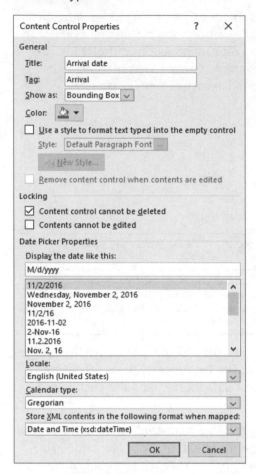

You can set the date format and locale for a date picker content control

The property Remove Content Control When Contents Are Edited can be set when you use a control to provide information about filling out information in the document, for example, but the content control is not needed when the document is completed and submitted. (This property is not available for every type of content control.)

Two properties you can set for controls help you protect the design and content of your document. The first property, Content Control Cannot Be Deleted, prevents a user of the document from deleting that control. You should set this property on every control that is required for the type of document you are creating. You can also set a property that prevents users from editing the content of a control. This property is suitable for titles or other controls whose content should remain static, such as text controls that display standardized text. Many controls require users to enter text, choose an option, or select an option from a list. For controls such as these, you should not set the option to prevent the content of a control from being edited.

In the Content Control Properties dialog box, by selecting Use A Style To Format Text Typed Into The Empty Control, you can apply a style to the content in a control. You can choose a style from the Style list (a limited number of styles are included) or click New Style in the Content Control Properties dialog box to open the Create New Style From Formatting dialog box.

See Also For information about creating styles, see "Objective 2.2: Create styles."

If you are working with a combo box or list box content control, the Content Control Properties dialog box includes fields that you use to define list items. In the Add Choice dialog box, which Word displays when you click Add in the list properties area, you specify the display name and value for each list item.

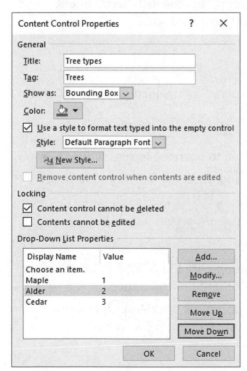

In the Drop-Down List Properties area, set up and organize list or combo box items

By default, Word repeats the text you enter in the Display Name box in the Value box (or vice versa, if you enter a value first). You can change the value to a numerical value, for example, to match a sequence of choices. Use the Modify button to make changes to the display names and values, and the Move Up and Move Down buttons to change the order of the items.

When you add content controls to a document, you can work in design mode. In design mode, Word displays tags that identify the content controls, and you can more easily arrange and edit the content controls in the document. When you insert a picture content control, however, you must turn off design mode before you can select the picture you want to display.

To turn design mode on or off

→ On the **Developer** tab, in the **Controls** group, click the **Design Mode** button.

To insert a text content control

1. Click where you want to insert the control.

2. On the **Developer** tab, in the **Controls** group, click the **Rich Text Content Control** button or the **Plain Text Content Control** button.

To insert a picture content control

1. Click where you want to insert the control.

2. On the **Developer** tab, in the **Controls** group, click the **Picture Content Control** button.

3. If design mode is on, turn it off.

4. In the picture content control, click the icon to open the **Insert Pictures** window.

5. From the **Insert Pictures** window, locate and select the picture you want to display.

To insert a combo box or a drop-down list

1. Click where you want to insert the control.

2. On the **Developer** tab, in the **Controls** group, click the **Combo Box Content Control** button or the **Drop-Down List Content Control** button.

3. With the content control selected in the document, click **Properties** in the **Controls** group to open the Content Control Properties dialog box.

4. In the **Drop-Down List Properties** area, click **Add**.

5. In the **Add Choice** dialog box, enter the display name and value of the first list item that you want to appear in the content control, and then click **OK**.

6. Repeat steps 4 and 5 to define each additional list item.

7. Select options for other properties, and then click **OK**.

To insert a date picker content control

1. Click where you want to insert the date picker control.

2. On the **Developer** tab, in the **Controls** group, click the **Date Picker Content Control** button.

3. With the content control selected in the document, click **Properties** in the **Controls** group to open the Content Control Properties dialog box.

4. In the **Date Picker Properties** area, select the date format you want to use, and change the settings for the locale and calendar type if necessary.

To insert a check box content control

1. Click where you want to insert the check box control.

2. On the **Developer** tab, in the **Controls** group, click the **Check Box Content Control** button.

3. With the content control selected in the document, click **Properties** in the **Controls** group to open the Content Control Properties dialog box.

4. In the **Check Box Properties** area, click the **Change** button to open the Symbol dialog box to select a different symbol for a selected or cleared check box.

To insert a building block gallery content control

1. Click where you want to insert the control.

2. On the **Developer** tab, in the **Controls** group, click the **Building Block Gallery Content Control** button.

3. With the content control selected in the document, click **Properties** in the **Controls** group.

4. In the **Content Control Properties** dialog box, select the gallery and category of building blocks that you want to make available in the content control, and then click **OK**.

4

To insert a repeating section content control

1. Select the content that you want to include in the control.

2. On the **Developer** tab, in the **Controls** group, click the **Repeating Section Content Control** button.

3. With the content control selected in the document, click **Properties** in the **Controls** group.

4. In the **Content Control Properties** dialog box, enter a section title, set other control properties, and then click **OK**.

To remove a content control from a document

→ Right-click the content control, and then click **Remove Content Control**.

To customize the text in a content control

1. Turn on design mode.

2. Select the content control you want to edit.

3. Edit the placeholder text, and apply any formatting you want.

4. Turn off design mode.

To lock a control

1. Select the content control, and on the **Developer** tab, in the **Controls** group, click **Properties**.

2. In the **Content Control Properties** dialog box, in the **Locking** area, select one or both of the following, and then click **OK**:

    -   **Content control cannot be deleted**
    -   **Contents cannot be edited**

To format a control

1. Select the content control, and on the **Developer** tab, in the **Controls** group, click **Properties**.

2. In the **Content Control Properties** dialog box, select the **Use a style to format text typed into the empty control** check box.

3. Do either of the following:

    -   In the **Style** list, click the existing style you want to apply to content in the control.
    -   Click **New Style** to open the **Create New Style from Formatting** dialog box. Define the attributes of the style and then click **OK**.

4. In the **Content Control Properties** dialog box, click **OK**.

Objective 4.1 practice tasks

The practice files for these tasks are located in the **MOSWordExpert2016 \Objective4** practice file folder. The folder also contains result files that you can use to check your work.

➤ Open the **WordExpert_4-1a** document, and do the following:

- ❑ Create a Quick Part from the "Executive summary" section of the document. Name the Quick Part Executive Summary, and accept the other defaults.

- ❑ Open the Building Blocks Organizer. Select the *Executive Summary* Quick Part and move it to a custom category named Report building blocks.

➤ Save the **WordExpert_4-1a** document. Open the **WordExpert_4-1a_ results** document. Compare the two documents to check your work. Then close the open documents.

➤ Open the **WordExpert_4-1b** document, place the cursor at the end of the "Financial results" section, and then record a macro named *PageSetup* that does the following:

- ❑ Inserts a Next Page section break.

- ❑ Sets the page orientation of the new section to Landscape.

- ❑ Immediately after the section break, inserts a table that has four columns and four rows.

- ❑ Adds column headings to the table for Quarter 1, Quarter 2, Quarter 3, and Quarter 4.

➤ Save the **WordExpert_4-1b** document. Open the **WordExpert_4-1b_ results** document. Compare the two documents to check your work. Then close the open documents.

➤ Open the **WordExpert_4-1c** document, and do the following:

- ❑ Under the existing text, add two plain-text content controls. Label the controls Name and Email Address.

- ❑ Under the plain-text controls, add a rich-text control. Label the control Shipping Address.

❏ Under the rich-text control, add a drop-down list content control that contains the list items <u>Small</u>, <u>Medium</u>, <u>Large</u>, and <u>Extra Large</u>. Label the drop-down list control <u>Jersey size</u>.

❏ Under the drop-down list control, add a plain-text control. Label the control <u>Billing address same as shipping address</u>. Set the properties to lock this control.

❏ Under the plain-text control, add a check box content control and sets its Title property to <u>Billing address same as shipping address</u>.

❏ To the right of the drop-down list box control, add a date picker content control. Change its label to <u>Preferred ship date</u>.

➤ Save the **WordExpert_4-1c** document. Open the **WordExpert_4-1c_ results** document. Compare the two documents to check your work. Then close the open documents.

Objective 4.2: Create custom style sets and templates

Templates, styles, and themes all provide ways to consistently format the content of a Word document. Templates contain styles and define settings for page layout and document elements such as headers and footers. Themes specify default fonts for body and heading text, colors for headings and other elements, and text effects such as shadows. Styles specify settings for fonts, paragraphs, tabs, and other formatting that are applied as a group to paragraphs and characters. Style sets provide a means of changing the appearance of multiple styles at one time. This topic describes how to create custom color and font sets, custom themes, and custom style sets.

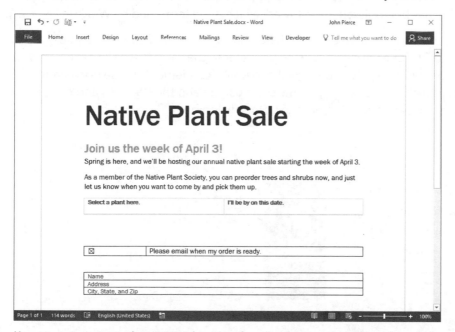

You can create your own themes to apply settings for colors, fonts, paragraph spacing, and other effects

See Also For more information about working with templates, see "Modify existing templates" in "Objective 1.1: Manage documents and templates." For more information about styles, see "Objective 2.2: Create styles."

When you work with themes, templates, styles, and style sets, keep in mind that a template is defined (in part) by the styles it contains and the attributes for those styles. After you apply styles to the content of your document, you can apply a different template or style set to update styles with the same name to reflect the formatting defined in the new template or style set. If the styles in a template or a document are set up to use theme fonts and theme colors, you can display a different set of fonts and colors by applying a new theme.

You manage themes and style sets by using commands in the Document Formatting group on the Design tab.

Create custom color and font sets

A color set specifies colors that are used to format elements such as text, backgrounds, accents, and hyperlinks. Accent colors appear in elements such as SmartArt graphics and banded tables. Text and background colors change formatting for elements such as headings and page backgrounds. Colors for hyperlinks vary depending on whether the hyperlink has been clicked (or followed, which is the term used by Word).

When you define a custom color set in the Create New Theme Colors dialog box, you can select a color for each element listed and refer to the Sample area to review how your selections will be applied to the text and graphical elements in the document. Color options include the existing theme color palette and the standard and custom color options that are available from the Colors dialog box.

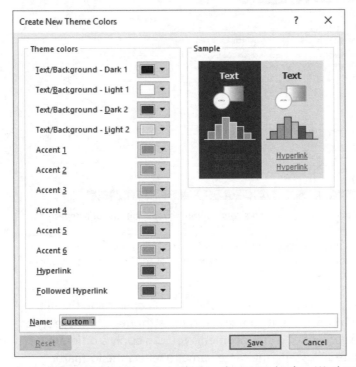

As you define a custom color set, use the Sample area to view how Word applies the colors

A font set includes a heading font and a body font. From the Fonts gallery on the Design tab, you can apply a font set to update the size and style of headings and other text in a document. You can create a font set of your own in the Create New Theme Fonts dialog box by selecting a heading font and a body font to use in combination.

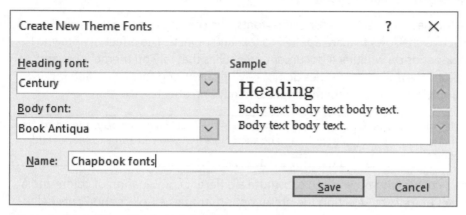

A font set can include any font that is installed on your computer

To create a custom color set

1. On the **Design** tab, in the **Document Formatting** group, click **Colors**, and then click **Customize Colors**.

2. In the **Create New Theme Colors** dialog box, click the color button to the right of any element for which you want to specify a color to display the menu of options.

3. In the theme color palette or standard color palette, click the color you want to assign to the element, or click **More Colors** to open the Colors dialog box, in which you can select from a greater number of standard colors or configure settings for a custom color.

4. Repeat steps 2 and 3 for each element whose color you want to change.

5. When you're done changing theme colors, enter a name for the collection of custom theme colors, and then click **Save**.

To create a custom font set

1. On the **Design** tab, in the **Document Formatting** group, click **Fonts**, and then click **Customize Fonts**.

2. In the **Create New Theme Fonts** dialog box, select the fonts you want to use for headings and for body text.

3. Enter a name for the set of custom theme fonts, and then click **Save**.

Create custom themes

Themes are used in Microsoft Office programs to apply formatting to elements throughout a document. By applying a theme, you can change the structure and appearance of document content.

In Word, themes affect settings for colors, fonts, line spacing in paragraphs, and effects such as shadows that are applied to text and objects. The effect of applying a theme depends on whether a document uses styles that rely on theme fonts and theme colors. If a document's styles do not rely on colors and fonts specified for themes, applying a different theme appears to have no effect.

Tip Word displays theme fonts in a separate section of the font list and displays theme colors together in the palettes available for fill and border colors that you can apply to shapes and other graphical objects.

To create a custom theme, you can substitute a different combination of colors and a different set of fonts by selecting the preset options from the Colors and Fonts galleries on the Design tab. You can also combine a custom set of colors, fonts, paragraph spacing, and effects as a theme. After applying the colors and other formatting that you want to include in the theme, save the theme to the Themes gallery.

To create a custom theme

1. In the active document, apply the color set, font set, paragraph spacing, and effects you want to include in the theme.
2. On the **Design** tab, click **Themes**, and then select **Save Current Theme**.
3. In the **Save Current Theme** dialog box, enter a name for the theme, and then click **Save**.

Create custom style sets

Style sets are like themes; they can change the overall appearance of a document in a single step. In addition to fonts and colors, style sets can change character attributes such as font size and capitalization, and paragraph attributes such as line spacing, borders, and alignment. The use of style sets reinforces the advantages of applying defined styles to distinct document elements (headings, lists, and normal paragraphs, for example). With styles in place in a document, you can change the look of a document by applying a different style set.

IMPORTANT Style sets change only formatting defined by styles. Any formatting applied directly to a document element is not updated by applying a style set.

A style set's definitions are contained in a .dotx file, the file name extension used for Word templates. However, applying a style set does not replace the template associated with a document; it only applies the style set's style definitions. If, after applying a style set, you want to restore the formatting defined in the current template, you can revert to using the style definitions included in that template by clicking the Reset command at the bottom of the Style Set gallery.

When you create and save a custom style set, Word prompts you to save the file in your user profile, at C:\Users*user name*\AppData\Roaming\Microsoft\QuickStyles.

See Also For more information about modifying styles, see "Modify styles" in "Objective 2.2: Create styles."

To create a custom style set

1. Set up a document with the style definitions you want to use. (Start with an existing style set if you want to.)

2. On the **Design** tab, in the **Document Formatting** group, click the **More** button to open the Style Set menu, and then click **Save as a New Style Set**.

3. In the **Save as a New Style Set** dialog box, name the style set, and then click **Save**.

4

Objective 4.2 practice tasks

The practice file for these tasks is located in the **MOSWordExpert2016 \Objective4** practice file folder. The folder also contains result files that you can use to check your work.

➤ Open the **WordExpert_4-2a** document, and do the following:

- ❑ Apply the *Savon* theme to the document.
- ❑ Apply the built-in *Green Yellow* theme color set to the document.
- ❑ Apply the built-in *Garamond* theme font set to the document.
- ❑ Observe how the font is applied to different elements and how the fonts change.
- ❑ Create a custom color set named <u>WordExpertColors.</u> Select *Lime* as the Accent 1 color.
- ❑ Create a custom font set named <u>WordExpertFonts.</u> Select *Century* as the heading font and *Bookman Old Style* as the body font.
- ❑ Observe how the font set is applied to different elements and how the fonts change.
- ❑ Apply the built-in *Black & White (Capitalized)* style set to the document and observe the changes.
- ❑ Modify the *Heading 1* style to use a font size of 22 pt., with a bold italic style.
- ❑ Modify the *Normal* style to use the Times New Roman font. Set the paragraph spacing to 12 pt. after. Save the changes as a custom style set named <u>WordExpertStyleSet</u>.

➤ Save the **WordExpert_4-2a** document.

➤ Open the **WordExpert_4-2a_results** document. Compare the two documents to check your work. Then close the open documents.

➤ Open the **WordExpert_4-2b** document.

- ❑ Apply the *WordExpertColors* custom color set.
- ❑ Apply the *WordExpertFonts* custom font set.
- ❑ Apply the *WordExpertStyleSet* custom style set.

➤ Save the **WordExpert_4-2b document**.

➤ Open the **WordExpert_4-2b_results** document. Compare the two documents to check your work. Then close the open documents.

Objective 4.3: Prepare a document for internationalization and accessibility

This topic describes procedures you can use to prepare a document for use by international (multilingual) readers and users with disabilities, and practices you can follow to help ensure that the content of a document meets general standards for internationalization and accessibility.

Configure language options in documents

When you install Office (or Word as a standalone program), it is configured by default to use one specific language. The spelling and proofing features in Word use this language when you check the spelling of a document, for example.

To work with documents that contain content in multiple languages, you can add other editing languages that Word can use when it checks spelling. You install additional languages from the Language page of the Word Options dialog box. After you install an editing language, it is available for any document you work with in Word.

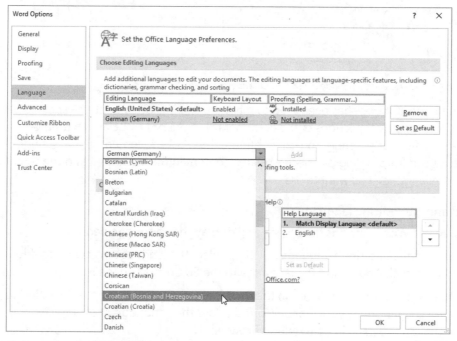

It's easy to install additional editing languages

When you are working in a document, you can specify the language of selected text and then check spelling by using that language. The proofing tools for the language you select must be installed to check the spelling in that language. By default, Word prompts you if the proofing tools are missing and provides a link for downloading the tools if they are available. The installed editing languages are marked at the top of the dialog box with the spelling icon.

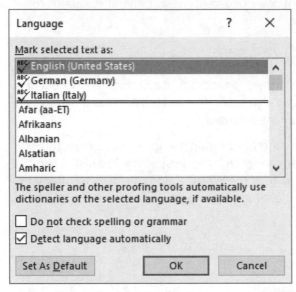

Mark selected text as a specific language to use that language's proofing tools

If more than one language has been used to mark the text in a document, the spelling checker might skip over portions of the document that are not associated with the language specified for proofing. You can configure the whole document so that a single language is used for proofing by selecting all the content in the document and then selecting the language you want to use.

To install another editing language

1. Open the **Word Options** dialog box and display the **Language** page.

2. In the **Choose Editing Languages** section, select the language you want to add, and then click **Add** to add the language to the Editing Language list.

3. In the list of editing languages, in the **Proofing** column, click the **Not Installed** link for the language you added. Word displays the Language Accessory Pack For Office 2016 page in your default browser.

4. In the **Step 1: Install the language accessory pack** area, select the editing language from the list.

5. In the **Links** column of the table that appears, click the **Download (x86)** or **Download (x64)** link, whichever one is appropriate for the operating system installed on your computer.

6. Follow the browser-specific prompts to download and install the proofing tools.

To set the proofing language for document content

1. Press **Ctrl+A** to select the whole document.

2. On the **Review** tab, in the **Language** group, click **Language**, and then click **Set Proofing Language**.

3. In the **Language** dialog box, select the language you want to use to proof the document, and then click **OK**.

IMPORTANT If you haven't already installed the proofing tools for the language you select, Word prompts you to do so.

---

4. Follow the standard process to check spelling.

Add alt text to document elements

Alt text (short for *alternative text*) is a description that you provide for an image or another type of graphical object (such as a table) to convey the information that the object depicts. If the image or object is not displayed or the user cannot view it (because of a visual disability, for example), the alt text you define provides a description of the information shown in the image.

You add alt text to images from the Layout And Properties page of the Format *Object* pane. (The name of the pane differs depending on the type of object involved—a picture, SmartArt object, or shape, for example.)

Alt text descriptions help people using a screen reader understand the content of visual objects

Use the Title field to identify the image and the Description field to provide details about the image's content. The title can be read to a user by a screen reader, and the user can then indicate whether to hear the full description.

Tip You can create a shortcut to the Format pane by adding the Alt Text command to the Quick Access Toolbar.

To add alt text to an image

1. Right-click the picture, and then click **Format Picture**.

2. In the **Format Picture** pane, click the **Layout and Properties** button.

3. Expand the **Alt Text** area if it is hidden, and then do the following:

   a. In the **Title** box, enter a simple description of the image.

   b. Optionally, in the **Description** box, enter a detailed description of the image.

To add alt text to a table

1. Do either of the following to open the Table Properties dialog box:

   • Right-click the table, and then click **Table Properties**.

   • Click in or select the table, and then on the **Layout** tool tab, in the **Table** group, click **Properties**.

2. In the **Table Properties** dialog box, on the **Alt Text** tab, do the following:

   a. In the **Title** box, enter a simple description of the table content.

   b. Optionally, in the **Description** box, enter a detailed description of the table content.

3. In the **Table Properties** dialog box, click **OK**.

Manage multiple options for the +Body and +Heading fonts

In many of the built-in styles in Word, the font is specified as Body (for styles such as Normal) or as Heading (for the built-in heading styles). The fonts associated with these generic designations are set by the document's theme. If you apply a different theme that uses different body and heading fonts, Word changes the font to match those defined for the new theme.

You can make changes to the properties for these generic font references and to the attributes of styles that depend on them. These settings are retained when you change themes, which can apply a different set of body and heading fonts to the document's content. Some of the changes you can make can help make a document easier to understand and more accessible. For example, you can change from a colored font for headings to the Automatic setting to make text more legible to a person who is colorblind.

To change properties for the styles that use body and heading font settings, you can work with settings on the Set Defaults tab of the Manage Styles dialog box.

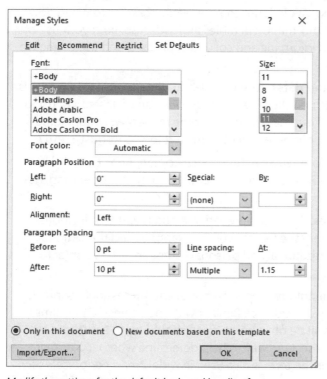

Modify the settings for the default body and heading fonts

To specify font settings for the body and heading fonts

1. Open the **Styles** pane.
2. At the bottom of the **Styles** pane, click the **Manage Styles** button.
3. In the **Manage Styles** dialog box, click the **Set Defaults** tab.
4. In the **Font** list, select **+Body** or **+Headings**, and then specify the settings for font size and font color (in addition to settings for position and spacing).
5. Click **OK**.

Implement global content standards

When you create documents that will be read, revised, and analyzed by international audiences, you should implement standards that make the document's content easy to understand. Some of the areas you need to consider are the use of jargon and technical terms, the type of examples you provide, and the syntax of sentences.

The following list describes these and other general standards you can follow in preparing content for an international audience:

- **Use global English syntax.** Avoid long, complex sentences. Try to break down and present complicated information in tables and lists. Also, limit your use of sentence fragments, avoid idiomatic and colloquial phrases, and use the active voice as much as possible.

- **Vary references to time and dates.** Use the 24-hour time format (13:00 equals 1:00 P.M., for example). Include the time zone for event times. Instead of using numerals for months, spell out month names. Some readers will understand 03/08/17 as March 8, 2017, but others will assume it refers to August 3, 2017.

- **Use standard fonts.** Use fonts such as Times New Roman, Arial, Courier New, and Verdana, which are available in browsers and on computer operating systems throughout the world.

- **Provide a mix of examples.** If you are preparing a document that includes examples and scenarios, vary the location of the examples and the national/regional identities of organizational and personal names and other contact information.

- **Avoid jargon.** Some terminology used in technical and professional contexts will be well understood by an audience familiar with the subject. Other times, this type of terminology will be obscure, and you should try to substitute a more familiar word or phrase. One way to help determine whether a term is jargon is to check whether the term is also used in widely read periodicals such as newspapers and magazines.

- **Strive for consistency in terminology and word choice.** Being precise and consistent in how specific terms are used aids understanding.

Objective 4.3 practice tasks

The practice files for these tasks are located in the **MOSWordExpert2016 \Objective4** practice file folder. The folder also contains result files that you can use to check your work.

➤ Open the **WordExpert_4-3a** document.

   ❑ Run the spelling checker to discover the spelling errors in the document.

   ❑ Set the proofing language for the whole document to English (United States), and then run the spelling checker again. Notice any errors that were skipped in the previous step.

➤ Save the **WordExpert_4-3a** document.

➤ Open the **WordExpert_4-3a_results** document. Compare the two documents to check your work, and then close the open documents.

➤ Open the **WordExpert_4-3b** document. Add alt text to the images, diagram, and table.

➤ Save the **WordExpert_4-3b document**.

➤ Open the **WordExpert_4-3b_results** document. Compare the two documents to check your work. Then close the open documents.

Index

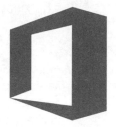

A

absolute positioning of objects 57–58
accepting changes 35
accessibility, adding alt text 141–142
address blocks
    inserting merge fields 105
    modifying 103
address lists
    compiling in Excel 97
    creating/managing 100
    editing 102
    filtering 98–99
    finding specific numeric values 99
    matching fields with merge fields 106
    modifying 100–102
    Outlook contacts, building from 100
    selecting external data sources 101
    sorting 98
    Word tables, building from 99
All Markup 34
alt text, adding 141–142
anchoring objects 58
asterisk (*), as wildcard character 43
at sign (@), as wildcard character 43
AutoCaption 89
automark files 77–78
AutoRecover 8
autosaved versions 10

B

background color, comment balloons 31
Body style, font settings for 142–143
book fold 51

book organization viii
bookmarks
    mail-merge rules 107
    page ranges in indexes 77
brackets ([ ]) as wildcard characters 43
breaks
    column 51
    page 51
    section 48–49
building block gallery 124
building block gallery content control 129
building blocks
    See also Quick Parts
    deleting 120
    galleries 115
    inserting 116
    location 7
    moving to different templates 7
    moving to documents 8
    naming 115
    properties 119
    Quick Parts 114–116
    save location 115–116
Building Blocks Organizer 7, 118–120

C

captions
    creating 91
    inserting 88–89
    modifying 89
    numbering 89
    outline levels 85
    positioning 88
    table of figures 90

W

About the author

JOHN PIERCE is a freelance editor and writer. He is the author of *Team Collaboration: Using Microsoft Office for More Effective Teamwork* and other books about Microsoft Office, including the *MOS 2013 Study Guide for Microsoft Word Expert*. John was an editor at Microsoft Press for 10 years and later worked as a technical writer at Microsoft, specializing in Microsoft SharePoint business solutions.

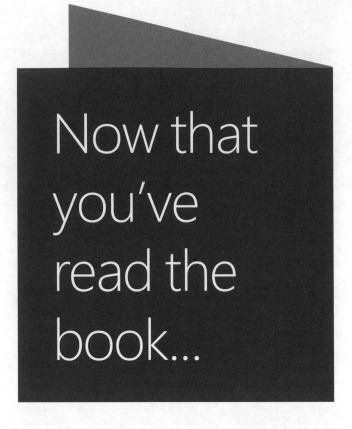

Now that you've read the book...

Tell us what you think!

Was it useful?
Did it teach you what you wanted to learn?
Was there room for improvement?

Let us know at https://aka.ms/tellpress

Your feedback goes directly to the staff at Microsoft Press,
and we read every one of your responses. Thanks in advance!